SEDUCING
AND KILLING
NAZIS

SEDUCING
AND KILLING
NAZIS

Hannie, Truus and Freddie:
Dutch Resistance Heroines of WWII

SOPHIE POLDERMANS

SWW Press (Sophie's Women of War Press)

The book was translated from Dutch into English by Gallagher Translations and Sophie Poldermans.

Front cover photos: (top, left to right) Jo (Hannie) Schaft, 1943 (photo by Cas Oorthuys); Freddie Oversteegen, 1945; (middle) Truus Oversteegen with Sten gun, WWII. These three old portraits are all Courtesy of North Holland Archives; (bottom, left to right) gravestone of Jo (Hannie) Schaft, 2018 (photo by Sophie Poldermans); Truus Menger-Oversteegen at an exhibition of her art work at North Holland Archives, May 3, 2008 (photo by Jaap Pop); Freddie Dekker-Oversteegen, 2000 (photo by Maarten Poldermans).

Back cover photo: Sophie Poldermans, Haarlemmerhout, 2018 (photo by Jaap Pop).

Interior illustration credits appear on pages xiii-xix.

Print ISBN: 978-9-08300-340-5

eBook ISBN: 978-9-08300-341-2

PRINTED IN THE UNITED STATES OF AMERICA

www.sophieswomenofwar.com

www.seducingandkillingnazis.com

To Sabine

"You shouldn't ask a soldier how many people he shot. I was also a soldier, a little one, a child soldier, but I was a soldier."

—Freddie Oversteegen

"If you have to make a decision, that decision must be a right one and you must always remain human."

—Truus Oversteegen

In My Mind's Eye

In my mind's eye, I see you all
still clear as day

no tears wash that away
no present fades the picture

… and yet, I felt the beat
of new life, in my life

and once again a tower of yelling
cheering children outside

no tears wash them away
no past can fade them
they are the ones to bear the future!

—Truus Menger-Oversteegen,
from *Op het netvlies van mijn denken (In My Mind's Eye)*, 2010

Contents

Illustrations

Preface

A S THE DAUGHTER OF AN ARCHAEOLOGIST AND A human geographer, historical awareness and the importance of humanity were instilled in me. I was taught to always treat another person equally and with respect, whether the person was a cleaner or a manager, a man or a woman, regardless of their cultural, economic or social background. I was taught to embrace and cherish freedom and to seize opportunities to develop myself. These were the ingredients of a strong sense of justice that were rooted in me from an early age.

Hannie Schaft was 19 years old when the Second World War broke out. Together with sisters Truus and Freddie Oversteegen, who were 16 and 14 years old at that time, Hannie Schaft was one of the few young women— girls still—who took up arms against the enemy in order to honor the ideal of a livable world.

I have always cherished the ideals of these three young women. They run like a common thread through my personal and professional life. I was Freddie's age (14) when I read Harry Mulisch's novel, *The Assault*. This novel is about a family in the city of Haarlem, 12 miles west of the Dutch capital Amsterdam, in the Netherlands. This family is confronted with an attack on a collaborating police chief during the Dutch famine or "Hunger

Winter" of 1944–1945 and is torn apart by the subsequent reprisals of the Germans. I was immediately fascinated by the injustice of the Nazi regime. I studied the Second World War in Haarlem and also the resistance fighter Hannie Schaft, who was the model for the main character of Mulisch's novel.

I was captivated by Hannie Schaft's life story and could certainly identify with her. I was also a teenager growing up in Haarlem, although fortunately under very different circumstances than Hannie. I started researching her life and her resistance work, which introduced me to the Oversteegen sisters.

When I was Truus' age (16), I had to write a thesis for my history class in high school on a self-chosen topic. For me, that topic was obvious: Hannie Schaft. I was very dedicated and dove into the subject. When I discovered Truus' contact details and called her up for an interview, she was so kind to invite me over. I remember that visit on a cold morning in February like it was yesterday. Truus could easily have been my grandmother, feeding me cookies and asking me if I liked her new glasses. But underneath that granny surface lay a whole different world. Her hand that shook mine when she invited me in, had held a gun, a gun that she had actually used to kill people. Although her targets were the enemy, they were people nevertheless. Over tea, she started telling me her story and that of Hannie and her sister Freddie, emphasizing its value for future generations, like mine.

When I submitted my final thesis to the National Hannie Schaft Commemoration Foundation, I was chosen at Truus' request, to be the keynote speaker at the annual Hannie Schaft Commemoration in 1998. When my speech was addressed as expressing the strength of womanhood, I knew that I was thirsty for more and wanted to further deepen my research. I got acquainted with Freddie, who told me her side of the story and who encouraged me to continue my exploration.

When I was Hannie's age (19), I started law school in Amsterdam, because just like her, I was interested in international law and the role of the United Nations in the setting of international peace and justice. At Truus' invitation, I joined the board of the National Hannie Schaft Commemoration Foundation (now the National Hannie Schaft Foundation). During these years as a board member, I got to know Truus and Freddie (both board members at the time) very well and was able to learn a great deal from them.

I knew both women for almost 20 years and worked closely with them for over a decade. I always admired these women for their strength, for their ability to look ahead and for their continuing faith in humanity, despite their own experiences and sacrifices.

How do you stay human in inhuman circumstances? As I was pondering this question, immediately another difficult question arose as to what I would have done if I had grown up in circumstances similar to theirs. This was the beginning of a personal quest for identity, for answers to moral questions and for evolving intrinsic leadership skills.

During my law studies, I developed an interest in wars and all its facets. On the one hand, I became fascinated by the fact that people are evidently capable of committing crimes against humanity. On the other hand, I drew hope from the fact that in such circumstances, there are always people who go to extraordinary lengths in order to embrace their ideals, to combat injustice and to believe in mankind.

We live in a world still dominated by men. As far as wars are concerned, women are often portrayed as the main victims, while it is often precisely women who resist under such circumstances and show genuine leadership.

In a globalizing world, we meet more and more people from different backgrounds, people who have fled from wars. Let us not exclude these people but, rather, take them into our midst and listen to their stories.

From a legal perspective with a multi-disciplinary approach, I have further explored the role of women in times of war. It is exactly these women who deserve our attention.

After living and travelling all around the world, I recently moved back to Haarlem with my family. Sitting at my writing desk, I can see the Haarlemmerhout from my window, the spot where Hannie, Truus and Freddie seduced high-ranking Nazi officers, lured them into the woods and killed them. These three young women never saw themselves as heroines, they did what they did "because it had to be done," because they believed in justice and because they never let go of their ideals. Across from my desk stands one of Truus' miniature sculptures of "Woman in Resistance," depicting Hannie Schaft, on an antique side table. I look at it every day, reminding me that we need strong female role models. We did then, we do now and we will in the future.

Prologue

THEY WERE STILL TEENAGE GIRLS—HANNIE SCHAFT, AND sisters Truus and Freddie Oversteegen. They should have been experimenting with their hair and makeup and gossiping about boys, like so many of their peers. Instead, they grew up during the Nazi regime of the Second World War, carrying a great responsibility on their shoulders. Immediately, they were deprived of their childhood and were forced to make decisions that did not fit their age and character. They faced a question far beyond what was expected of them: to adapt or to resist?

During the Second World War, relatively few people were active in the Dutch resistance against the German occupiers. The majority of the Dutch population, an estimated 90 percent, tried to continue to live their lives as normal as possible. Listening to the illegal radio station "Radio Oranje" and reading illegal newspapers were forms of passive resistance that most people related to.

A small part of the population, about 5 percent, consisted of collaborators. They betrayed people in hiding and worked together with the German occupying forces.

The remaining 5 percent of the Dutch population were engaged in active resistance. This form of resistance consisted of printing and/or distributing illegal newspapers, helping people in hiding, collecting information for the government that fled to London or committing acts of sabotage. Only a small part of this group offered armed resistance, and the majority of those who did were men.

Hannie, Truus and Freddie were girls from completely different backgrounds and with totally distinct characters. So, what is it that this clever auburn-haired Hannie, the down-to-earth tomboy and natural leader Truus, and the feminine and fierce Freddie had in common? They honored the same ideals regarding a livable world and felt compelled by the inhuman conditions of the German occupation to take up arms against the enemy in order to fight injustice. They were some of the very few women who offered armed resistance in the Netherlands. After her execution, Hannie Schaft became an icon of the Second World War just like Anne Frank. Whereas Anne Frank's story is one of survival, Hannie Schaft became the icon of women's resistance.

In 2020, it will be 75 years since the Netherlands was liberated from German occupation, and it will be 100 years since Hannie Schaft was born. This was a long time ago, so why is it important to remember and reflect on the meaning of the concept of freedom today? Freedom is not as self-evident as it might seem. People are still excluded and discriminated against every day. There is always a war going on somewhere in the world, and sadly enough there probably always will be.

This book is a non-fiction account of historical events, can be categorized as a historical biography and can serve as a reference guide. I deliberately chose this genre to give a chronological account of the specific events that took place as precisely as possible. In this way, I hope that the stories of these young women can be handed down accurately to future generations.

The method I used for the compilation of this book was twofold: qualitative research of available sources and as much first-hand information as possible that I could obtain by conducting interviews and conversations with those who were directly involved.

In this book, I will try to depict the lives and resistance work of Hannie Schaft, and sisters Truus and Freddie Oversteegen. I will explain how these three young women worked together in their mission to fight the enemy and what impact that had on their lives. Finally, I will give you an insight into how their resistance work was perceived after the war and how it can still inspire people today. In doing so, I will try to shed light on the questions of how a person remains human under inhuman conditions and why it is vital to remember and cherish freedom in today's world.

Awareness is the first step toward understanding people and society, and it is crucial for learning from (earlier) mistakes. Knowledge and education can function as a form of empowerment and as a catalyst for hope and change, serving as a gateway toward human connection and global understanding.

I hope this book will enrich and inspire you, will make you aware of the dangers of exclusion in the broadest sense of the word, and will challenge you to take a moment to ask yourself "What would I have done if I had been in the shoes of Hannie, Truus or Freddie?"

PART I

EARLY DAYS

Chapter 1

Jo (Hannie) Schaft's Childhood

JANNETJE JOHANNA SCHAFT WAS BORN ON SEPTEMBER 16, 1920 in the city of Haarlem, in the Netherlands. Haarlem is the capital of the province of North Holland and is located 12 miles west of the country capital Amsterdam. Jannetje's nickname was Jo or Jopie. Hannie was the name she used while she was working in the resistance, and the name by which she became famous.

Jo grew up in a close-knit family. Jo's father, Pieter Claasz. Schaft, worked in education and was an active member of the Social Democratic Workers Party (SDAP). Her mother, Aafje Talea Johanna Vrijer, also worked in education until she married Pieter, ending her career in order to devote herself entirely to her family. Jo had a sister, Annie, who was five years older. At the age of 12, Annie died of diphtheria on December 6, 1927. Annie's death was a terrible blow to the Schaft family, one from which they never completely recovered.

The Schaft family moved within Haarlem several times while Jo was growing up. In 1923, they lived at Anslijnstraat 49. In 1926, they moved to Rozenhagenplein 13. In 1929 or 1930, the family moved to Wouwermanstraat 75. Finally, in 1936, they moved to Van Dortstraat 60.[1]

Jo went to the Tetterodeschool for primary school. She loved school and was an excellent student at the top of her class, a fact her parents were very proud of. But, in spite of this, Jo was shy and withdrawn, and she was often bullied because of her red hair and freckles.

Various interviews and surviving materials have revealed an image of a family that was very socially committed but, partly due to the tragedy of Annie's death, lived a relatively secluded life. The family survived the global economic crisis of 1929 reasonably well.

After Annie died, Jo's parents became very protective of her. In 1932, when Jo started high school, she was not allowed to go to the Stedelijk Gymnasium at the Prinsenhof in the city center because the bike ride would be too long. Instead, she went to the second HBS-B high school at the Santpoorterplein near their home. Jo also excelled as a high school student and was highly intelligent, but she had little connection with her classmates; her parents' overprotectiveness cemented her place as an out-sider. Miep Merkuur, a school friend of Jo, remembers that even when it was very hot, Jo had to wear a thick cardigan, because her parents were afraid that she would catch a cold.[2]

At the Schaft family dinner table, politics was a recurring topic of con-versation and the developments in Germany, as Adolf Hitler came to power, were closely followed. The family had concerns about Hitler and his National Socialism but also about Anton Mussert, the leader of the National Socialist Movement (NSB) in the Netherlands.

Without knowing what her future would hold, Jo made a drawing in kin-dergarten depicting a house with the word *Peace* written on the facade.[3] Jo's parents taught her about such principles as justice and equality, lessons that were evident from the essays Jo wrote in school. A good example of this is a piece she wrote about the atrocities committed by the Italians in Abyssinia under the leadership of Benito Mussolini.[4]

After Jo passed her final exams in 1937, she initially wanted to become a Dutch language teacher, however she decided against teaching because she dreaded keeping order in the classroom. Instead, because justice was such an important value for Jo, she decided to study law at the University of Amsterdam. Jo specialized in international law and her dream was to go to Geneva after graduating to join the League of Nations (the forerunner of the United Nations). Working at the League of Nations would enable her to apply her ideals of justice and equality into practice.[5]

During her law school days, she developed more social contacts, but she remained a quiet, shy girl. She became a member of the Amsterdam Female Student Association (AVSV) and made friends with two Jewish girls, Philine Polak and Sonja Frenk. Two other girls, Annie van Calsem and Nellie Luyting, also belonged to her group of friends. With Annie and Nellie, she founded GEMMA within the AVSV in December 1940. Another friend, Erna Kropveld, joined the group as well. GEMMA stood for *Gemmare e minoribus appetinus*, which is Latin for "From small things we strive for bigger things."[6]

Kindergarten drawing by Jo (Hannie) Schaft:
Villa Peace. (Courtesy of North Holland Archives)

Kindergarten drawing by Jo (Hannie) Schaft:
family dinner table. (Courtesy of North Holland Archives)

Schaft Family: Jo (Hannie) is the smallest child.
(Courtesy of North Holland Archives)

Van Dortstraat 60, 2018: parental home of
Jo (Hannie) Schaft from 1936. (Photo by Sophie Poldermans)

High school graduation class of Jo (Hannie) Schaft, showing Jo standing in the front row, on the far right. (Courtesy of North Holland Archives)

Chapter 2

Jo (Hannie) Schaft's First Acts of Resistance

AFTER THE GERMAN INVASION OF POLAND ON SEPTEMBER 1, 1939, Jo believed something had to be done. For months she sent parcels containing food, clothing and blankets via the International Red Cross to imprisoned Polish officers.[7]

The following spring, on May 10, 1940, German troops invaded the Netherlands. Jo went to stay with her parents in Haarlem, where they followed reports of the invasion anxiously, especially the fleeing of Queen Wilhelmina and the government to London and the bombardment of the city of Rotterdam 50 miles south of Haarlem. On May 15, the Netherlands surrendered, but just three days later, on May 18, Haarlem born Bernard IJzerdraat was one of the first who called for resistance in his piece "Geuzenbericht," in the newspaper of the resistance organization "De Geuzen," in Rotterdam.[8]

After the turmoil of the invasion subsided, Jo went back to Amsterdam and soon everyday life continued as usual. Jo visited with her Jewish friends, Philine and Sonja, and resumed her studies, while living with Annie and

Nellie at Michelangelostraat 59 in Amsterdam. Of course, the girls discussed the German occupation and the related tensions. They often had dinner at the students' association, listened to the illegal radio station "Radio Oranje" and read illegal university newspapers.[9]

In October 1940, all government officials, including professors and lecturers at the university, were required to sign an "Aryan declaration" (proof of Germanic origin), an act that could be regarded as one of the first signs of the systematic exclusion of Jews. It is noteworthy that most of the officials signed this declaration. A month later, on November 22, Jews were permanently expelled from universities. A strongly worded article appeared in the student magazine, *Propria Cures*, about the departure of Jewish professors and students, but student life more or less continued as usual. In Amsterdam, however, more and more fights broke out at Jewish businesses and shops, whose proprietors were then harassed and attacked.[10]

As a response to the first raids by the German occupiers, in which more than 400 Jewish men were arrested and deported, the "February Strike" took place on February 25, 1941. This event was the first large-scale act of resistance against the German occupation and represented a turning point; the February Strike was the only open protest on a massive scale against the persecution of Jews in occupied Europe, and it stirred up resistance throughout the Netherlands. Jo Schaft was also motivated to resist and took part in a number of protests. When stricter measures were announced against Jews in the autumn of 1941, Jo declared, "If they are no longer allowed to walk through the park, I will not go there anymore either."[11]

It was hard for Jo to keep studying while she was concerned about the fate of Philine and Sonja, for whom it became increasingly difficult to study and who were no longer allowed to be members of the student association. The AVSV stopped its activities, but the GEMMA fraternity still came together. Jo, as well as Annie and Nellie, began to struggle academically and scored poorly on their examinations. As a result, their parents withdrew their contribution toward rent of their room in Amsterdam, and in early 1942, Jo went back to live with her parents in Haarlem. Fortunately, Philine and Sonja still visited her regularly.[12]

Jo's resistance intensified after May 9, 1942, when the Jews were forced to wear a yellow star on their clothes in public. Jo began stealing identity cards from various public places where there were unguarded cloakrooms or changing rooms, places like swimming pools, theaters, concert halls and cafes. One of the places she frequented was the Stoops swimming pool in Overveen. Jo then gave these identity cards to Jews or to resistance organizations who would forge these vital identity papers. Jo's fellow student and friend, Erna Kropveld, was one of the people who forged identity cards. From Erna, we know that Jo was very driven and acted quickly: "If a personal identification card was needed for a woman of about 40 years of age, Jo would take care of it within an hour." Jo helped her Jewish friends Sonja and Philine, as well as others. Sonja, in particular, had to be very careful because she had dark facial features which could be described as stereotypically Jewish. Jo helped several Jewish girls, including Philine and Sonja, go into hiding, sometimes even letting them spend the night with her parents in Haarlem.[13]

In the winter of 1942–1943, universities, including the University of Amsterdam, suffered from several attacks and raids by the German occupiers. After February 6, 1943, every student had to sign a "declaration of loyalty" declaring "to observe the laws and regulations in force to the best of their knowledge and belief and to refrain from any action directed against the German Empire ..." This went too far for Jo and the GEMMA fraternity; they decided not to sign the declaration. They were not alone. Throughout the Netherlands, more than 85 percent of students refused to sign the declaration. As a result, university life was put almost entirely on hold. Lectures and exams were still given, although illegally, in special places. Jo probably took her exams in the restaurant of Amsterdam's Central Station, where she more or less completed her studies. She decided to continue living with her parents in Haarlem and asked her friends Philine and Sonja to move in with them.[14]

University student card of Jo (Hannie) Schaft. (Courtesy of North Holland Archives)

*GEMMA fraternity: Jo (Hannie) Schaft is standing center,
with a bouquet of flowers. (Courtesy of North Holland Archives)*

Jo (Hannie) Schaft as a student. (Courtesy of North Holland Archives)

Jo (Hannie) Schaft as a student near her parental home.
(Courtesy of North Holland Archives)

Windmill across from parental home of Jo (Hannie)
Schaft, 2018. (Photo by Sophie Poldermans)

German troops arrive at Grote Markt, Haarlem,
May 1940. (Courtesy of North Holland Archives)

Jo (Hannie) Schaft in 1943. (Photo by Cas Oorthuys,
Courtesy of North Holland Archives)

Jo (Hannie) Schaft in 1943. (Photo by Cas Oorthuys,
Courtesy of North Holland Archives)

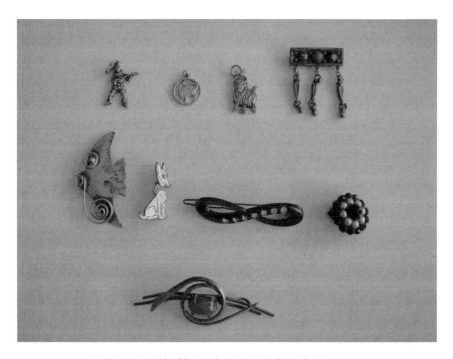

Jo (Hannie) Schaft's jewelry, 2013. (Photo by Maarten Poldermans, Courtesy of North Holland Archives)

Jo (Hannie) Schaft's purse, 2018. (Photo by Sophie Poldermans, private collection of Hannie Menger)

Chapter 3

Truus and Freddie
Oversteegen's Childhood

T RUUS OVERSTEEGEN WAS BORN ON AUGUST 29, 1923 IN Schoten, near Haarlem. Her sister, Freddie Nanda Oversteegen, was born on September 6, 1925 in Schoten as well. Freddie was named after a boy who was taken into their home as a foster child by Truus and Freddie's parents, who had died at the age of five.

In their early childhood, they lived with their parents Trijntje van der Molen (who also preferred being called Truus because she didn't like her name, but who will be referred to as Trijntje throughout this book in order to avoid confusion with her daughter, Truus) and Jacob Wilhelm Oversteegen (who was called Co) in several places in and around Haarlem. They moved many times, hopping from one eccentric place to another, including a houseboat, a horse wagon and a squatted building in Aerdenhout.

Father Oversteegen was a handsome and an imposing man with a beautiful voice. He could sing very well, but didn't do much else. He was out of a job most of the time and wanted to go wherever the wind blew him. This caused much tension within the family. Father Oversteegen not taking responsibility for his family finally caused a divorce in 1933, which was exceptional for that time. He remarried a year later, had two more children and spent the war years in the city of Ede in the central part of the Netherlands.

Trijntje van der Molen found herself in the uncommon role of single-mother, but rose to the circumstances. She took good care of her daughters, raising them to become independent women. Eventually they moved to the Nassaulaan 14, in Haarlem. Trijntje was originally a communist and was very active and socially involved. As early as 1934, Truus and Freddie's family offered—via the Committee de Rode Hulp—shelter to five Jewish people who had fled the Nazi regime in Germany: a woman with two sons (eight and ten years old), a Mr. Jered and a Ms. Frank. All this was done secretly, since providing shelter for such refugees was illegal in the Netherlands. The family made room for these people in their tiny workers' house.

"The first thing the Nazis took from Freddie Oversteegen was her bed," *The Observer* wrote on September 23, 2018, just after Freddie's death.[15] The same applied to Truus because they both slept in the same bed. But the sacrifice of their bed made room for Jewish refugees in hiding. It is important to note that in 1934 the Netherlands was not yet occupied by the Germans. The Nazis made life for Jewish people in Germany so difficult that many fled to safer countries, including to the Netherlands. The Oversteegens were one of the families who provided Jewish refugees with a safe house. Around this time, Trijntje gave birth to a son, Robbie. The father was unknown, but in all probability one of the men who had stayed at their house.

In the years that followed, political tension rose to extremely high levels in Europe, eventually resulting in the United Kingdom and France declaring war on Germany on September 3, 1939. (The war did not start until May 10, 1940 in the Netherlands when the German army invaded). Due to these tensions, the Jewish refugees in hiding with the Oversteegens were forced to stay in the Netherlands. Some refugees tried to flee to England by boat. Tragically, one of these boats, the *Simon Bolivar*, was bombed on November 18, 1939; the boat capsized and all the people in it drowned.[16]

Disaster almost struck for the Oversteegens themselves when the people hiding with them were found. One day, when the homeowner came to the door, one of the refugees, Mr. Jered, opened the door (despite Trijntje's express warning not to do so). When Mr. Jered replied in German, "Frau Van der Molen ist nicht da" ("Ms. Van der Molen is not home"), the house was immediately surrounded by Dutch policemen. Not only was it prohibited, as mentioned earlier, to offer shelter to illegal refugees but with everything that was going on in Germany, anyone who spoke German was considered suspicious. This meant they could be arrested by the Dutch authorities, both for speaking German and for being illegal refugees. Once the war started in 1940 and the Netherlands was occupied, German Jewish refugees were in even more danger because they risked being deported. Fortunately, in this particular instance, the Dutch policemen left without making any arrests or causing harm to the refugees.[17]

When the war broke out in the Netherlands, Truus and Freddie were 16 and 14 years old respectively. They lived with their mother Trijntje and their six-year-old half-brother Robbie in the Haarlem Leidsebuurt, among others, at Brouwersstraat 126 in 1940 and Olycanstraat 36 from 1940 until 1943.

From the beginning of the war, the Oversteegens printed illegal magazines in their living room with a stencil machine. The printing machine created such a noise that they had to be very careful not to attract attention. Robbie would stand as the lookout with a friend and would shout out "mama" whenever there were Germans around.[18] Truus and Freddie were often found on the streets drawing pro-resistance slogans on walls. That was the very beginning of their resistance.

op de foto voor mam's verjaardag
Robbie was toen nog geen 2 jaar

Truus and Freddie Oversteegen and their little brother Robbie van der Molen in 1935. Caption: "Photo taken for mother's birthday. Robbie was not even 2 years old." (Courtesy of North Holland Archives)

Brouwersstraat 126, 2018: parental home of Truus and Freddie Oversteegen in 1940. (Photo by Sophie Poldermans)

Olycanstraat 36, 2018: parental home of Truus and Freddie Oversteegen from 1940-1943. (Photo by Sophie Poldermans)

Trijntje van der Molen's stencil machine used to print illegal magazines,
2018. (Photo by Sophie Poldermans, private collection of Hannie Menger)

Chapter 4

Truus and Freddie Oversteegen's First Acts of Resistance

A T ONE POINT IN 1941, A MAN WEARING A HAT AND A grey suit came to the door, asking to see the girls. Truus and Freddie initially felt rather uncomfortable with this gentleman's visit and giggled, as only teenage girls can, at this fashionable stranger there to visit them. Freddie said of this visit: "To us came the men with the caps, not men with hats. This man looked like a movie star." The well-dressed gentleman was Frans van der Wiel, Regional Commander of the Council of Resistance (RVV) of Haarlem and its surrounding areas. He asked the two girls to participate in more serious forms of resistance, such as sabotage, and possibly even armed resistance. Truus was initially suspicious of this man and his request. Freddie became very nervous, and when asked if she could shoot someone to death, replied excitedly that she had never done anything like that before.[19]

The second time Truus and Freddie met with Frans again, they were surprised when he suddenly aimed a gun at them. He told the girls they had been set up and that he was from the Gestapo ("Secret State Polizei," political or secret state police of Nazi Germany). Aiming his pistol at them, Frans demanded the girls give him the address of a Jewish man. Truus and Freddie protested fiercely and started kicking and hitting Frans. Frans cried out that it was a test and that they had passed it brilliantly: they were found suitable for resistance work.[20]

Their mother, Trijntje, knew the girls were in the resistance, but she did not know exactly what they were doing. She made extensive inquiries to see if Frans van der Wiel could be trusted and was satisfied that he was; however, she was never told what her daughters' resistance work entailed. For safety reasons, she was not allowed to know and she did not want to know, either. When asked about this, Truus said, "She would have never approved it!"[21]

The fact that Truus and Freddie were still teenage girls was extremely beneficial to the resistance. Resistance work, especially armed resistance, was usually carried out by men. As young girls, they were less conspicuous than their older male counterparts.

Truus carried out resistance work under her own name. Freddie went by a form of her middle name, Nanni, before the war. When she joined the resistance, she thought it was better to have a boy's name. "Women do not go into resistance," she said in an interview, so she decided to do the work under her first name, Freddie.[22]

Both sisters took their assignments very seriously. The ideals their mother instilled in them, of justice and a livable world, were paramount. However, they had a very difficult task ahead of them: remaining human at all times, whatever they did.[23]

Frans van der Wiel, Regional Commander of the Council of Resistance (RVV)
of Haarlem and its surrounding areas, n.d. (Courtesy of North Holland Archives)

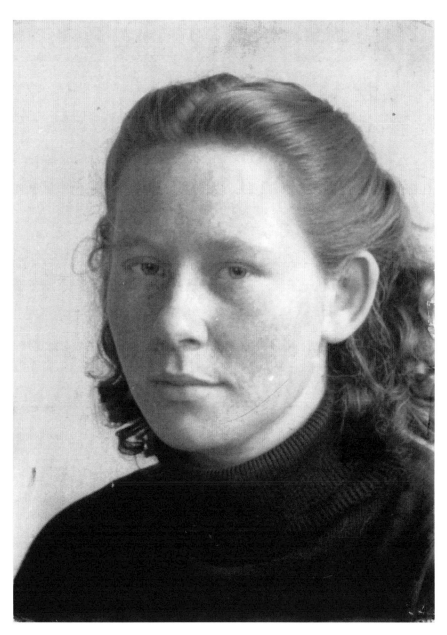

Truus Oversteegen in 1943. (Courtesy of North Holland Archives)

Truus Oversteegen in 1943. (Courtesy of North Holland Archives)

Freddie Oversteegen in 1943. (Courtesy of North Holland Archives)

Freddie Oversteegen in 1945. (Courtesy of North Holland Archives)

PART II

IN THE MIDST OF WAR

Chapter 5

Hannie, Truus and Freddie:
The Trinity of the Council of Resistance

I N THE SPRING OF 1943, JO SCHAFT REGISTERED WITH THE Council of Resistance (RVV). She told the council that helping people in hiding with money and vouchers was not enough for her. She wanted to offer more active resistance, "If necessary, with weapons."

Hannie's first assignment was to shoot an SD officer ("Sicherheits Dienst" or Security Service) with RVV member Cor Rusman. Though Jo was extremely scared of what was about to happen, when the time came, she pulled the trigger. However, instead of a shot, a click sounded. Nothing happened. The assignment had been a test. The SD officer came over to her and introduced himself as Frans van der Wiel, Commander of the RVV. Jo had passed the test, but she was furious at being put into a situation like that. Tears of outrage rolled down her cheeks.[24] Despite her indignation at the manner in which she was tested, she officially joined the RVV and from that moment on she carried out her resistance work under the name Hannie Schaft.

In the summer of 1943, Trijntje and Robbie had to leave Haarlem. By this time, their entire neighborhood knew they were printing illegal newspapers and offering shelter to Jewish people. It was no longer safe for them to stay in their home. Trijntje took Robbie to Enschede in the eastern part of the Netherlands, where Trijntje's sister Aunt Griet lived. A little later, they found a more permanent home in Epe, on the farm of Mr. Volkerink (a man whom Trijntje would marry after the war). That same summer, Truus and Freddie followed their mother and Robbie to Enschede; safety concerns had prompted the RVV members in Haarlem to split up and disappear for a time. In Enschede, Truus and Freddie worked as nurses in the Evacuation Hospital Twente.

The RVV used to work in teams and because Frans van der Wiel thought Hannie would pair up well with the Oversteegen sisters, Hannie was commissioned to contact Truus and Freddie. Hannie went to the hospital in Enschede disguised as a student nurse. Truus and Freddie's Aunt Griet was also a member of the resistance working in that same hospital; she introduced Hannie to Truus and Freddie as a friend. Hannie presented herself as Miss de Wit and told Truus and Freddie she had been sent by Frans (with no mention of his last name due to security reasons). The headmistress of the hospital gave the three young women her office for some privacy. Outside lay the ashes and ruins of heavy bombardments; inside it was quiet, damp, the curtains were pulled. The three young women sat down at the large table in the middle of the room across from each other. The tension in the room was so thick, one could cut it with a knife. The girls did not know if they could trust each other, each thought that the other might be a spy for the Germans and waited for the other to make the first move. Truus and Freddie had their guns ready, so did Hannie. No one spoke, silence lingered in the room for a prolonged amount of time as each tried to size the other up. Then, something changed. All of a sudden, they realized the absurdity of the situation and, as Truus pointed out, they started to laugh like crazy. Tears from releasing tension rolled down their cheeks and they roared with laughter because of the ludicrous situation. The ice was broken. Hannie put her gun on the table, and Truus and Freddie followed.[25]

Freddie explained in an interview that she was initially somewhat jealous of Hannie because she now had to share the special position that she and her sister had of being the only women in the RVV. Freddie commented: "At first sight, Hannie was a sweetheart and very gentle. If she seemed so soft at first, you would think, 'How is it possible that such a person is in the resistance?' We [Freddie and Truus] were in my mind much tougher than she was. We assumed wrong, as it quickly turned out. Hannie was a real resistance woman, very courageous and fiercely anti-fascist. And when she did her thing, you thought, 'Yes!'"[26] Slowly Freddie opened up, after which a close association arose between the three young women who often worked together in the context of the RVV. This bond of trust became so strong that a close friendship finally formed.

The three young women made a great team: Hannie was the lawyer, the intellectual. Truus was a decisive, down-to-earth leader. Freddie was the intelligence, the one who would explore and map everything out in advance.[27]

Hannie taught Truus and Freddie German and English. At first, Truus and Freddie refused to learn German, but Hannie made it clear to them that speaking German fluently was very important in their resistance work. When Truus and Freddie realized the value of knowing German, they finally agreed.

There was one clear advantage the three young women had over their male colleagues: their youth and beauty, which they used as a secret "weapon." One of their missions was to act as "Moffen girls." "Moffen girls" were Dutch girls who had (alleged) relationships with German soldiers. "Mof" was a Dutch derogatory term to indicate a German soldier, similar to "Kraut" in English. They would dress up nicely, powder their faces, extend their eyelashes with mascara and apply shiny eyeshadow and colorful lipstick to appear as attractive as possible. The trio had a great laugh about these experiences. Truus laughed as she later explained she had never worn makeup before. But the girls had help; Freddie explained that Frans van der Wiel did their makeup, "With those bright red lips, we looked ridiculous. Men can't do that, can they?" she said with a smile.[28] The girls would chat, giggle and flirt with German soldiers and high-ranking officers in order to coax information out of them or, later on, to seduce them and lure them into the woods to eventually kill them.

The RVV originated from the *Waarheid* ("Truth") group (communist resistance magazine). Under Frans van der Wiel, the group developed into a branch of armed resistance, starting with sabotage missions. Initially, the work was mainly done with "fireboxes" (small fire bombs), but later expanded to include firearms. The equipment that the group worked with was often of poor quality and as a result, a number of well-prepared actions failed.[29]

The RVV consisted of a permanent core of about seven people with an additional five who carried out tasks for the group on demand.

Jan Heusdens was part of the RVV. He described Hannie as follows: "There she was, a pitiful figure actually, a skittish bird, well dressed, but then you think, 'How does Frans get it in his head to bring such a person to us? Does she know what we are doing? [...]'. Afterward, that wasn't as bad as expected at all [...]. She didn't say a lot, but when it comes to the real thing, when it comes to performance, wise words did come out and you could see that she knew exactly what she was doing. That she was a real tough one, she wanted to push on, and work fanatically on the job. Someone who gives the impression that she has a sharp tongue, someone who knows very well what she is doing. That gives a great deal of confidence."[30]

Frans van der Wiel wrote in a written statement after the war, "Hannie more and more turned out to be a courageous, enthusiastic girl who sometimes had to be restrained a bit for her own safety."[31]

The headquarters of the RVV were located at Wagenweg 244–246, where the Haarlem sculptor Mari Silvester Andriessen (1897–1979) lived. The headquarters were next door to the "Huis met de beelden," the "House with the Statues," which was well known to many Haarlem residents. Hannie, Truus and Freddie hid there many times. As the war continued and safety concerns escalated, the group later met at various other places.[32]

Early on, the women's resistance work consisted mainly of the distribution of illegal material, such as newspapers but later included distribution of weapons, theft and forgery of identity cards and acts of sabotage. Truus remembered that blowing up a freight train was one of the missions that gave her the most satisfaction.[33]

In addition to coaxing information out of German soldiers, they also mapped out part of the coastal defenses, the Atlantic Wall (more than 5,000 kilometers of a defense line constructed by the Germans in the occupied territories against possible invasion by the Allies) in IJmuiden. This information was then forwarded to the government in London, information which would later allow the Allied bombing of the German defenses. Additionally, the girls managed to get details about the location of a V1 launch site. V1 stood for "Vergeltungswaffe 1" or Vengeance Weapon 1 and was a kind of unmanned flying bomb deployed by the Germans for terror bombing of London. They ensured that this information was passed on to the government in London as well.

Their resistance work also included the liquidation of dangerous Germans and Dutch people, including members of the SS ("Schutz Staffel," or Protection Squadron), the SD and the NSB. Freddie later said with a smile, "Oh well, liquidation is a nice word for killing."[34]

It all started with Truus' assignment to dress up as a "Moffen girl," to pick up a high-ranking German SS officer from a bar on the Houtplein, and to lure him into the woods under the guise of taking a romantic walk. Freddie would be on watch. Frans would walk behind them and shoot the SS officer through his head. Truus remembered her aversion to the assignment, which made her nauseous; this was the first time she and Freddie had taken on such a mission. Despite their nerves, Truus played her role perfectly and Frans succeeded in liquidating the officer. The relief of completing the mission was to be short-lived, however. Suddenly, they heard German trucks arriving and dogs barking. They had to get out of the forest quickly and ran out as fast as they could, accidentally leaving Freddie, who had been standing at a tree as the lookout, behind. Truus climbed over the fence near the tennis courts and escaped. Later, she went back to look for Freddie, who was still standing there, shaking like a leaf at the same tree; she had urinated in her pants.[35]

In the beginning, liquidations took place in public, according to Frans van der Wiel. However, when retaliations by the Germans followed, Frans decided that liquidations had to take place somewhere they were less likely to be noticed, such as in or near the Haarlemmerhout (the city forest). He could then transport the bodies of their targets using a cargo bike with a tarp over it to the forest and hide them there. Frans said, "This was a lugubrious job, but I hardened myself because I was fighting for a good cause." This method also proved to be too risky because of possible retaliations, so Frans decided to use the young women from his resistance group as "Moffen girls" so that they could lure the officers and other high-ranking Germans into the forest and then liquidate them there.[36]

In the yard of the "House with the Statues" and the surrounding Haarlemmerhout, the young women had shooting lessons. They could then use the same tactics and lure their German targets into the Haarlemmerhout to liquidate them. Freddie explained, "We only shot *real* traitors. When you see someone fall, your natural instinct is to pick them up."[37] A little later she added, "We did not bury them; the tough men did that."[38]

In addition to shooting lessons in the Haarlemmerhout, the three young women also received weapon instructions from a dentist at the Kloppersingel. Truus said this about their training: "We were three young girls, who laughed off most of our anxiety…For example, we always went into the dentist's house at the back. One day it was agreed that we would ring the bell at the front. But we had made a mistake with the house. When the door opened, we saw a very large portrait of Hitler hanging in the hallway. We thought this was such a stupid situation that we just cracked up. The woman stared at us with her mouth wide open. We quickly ran away. We laughed for quite a while around the corner."[39]

Once, when a high-ranking German SS officer was lured to the forest by Truus and Freddie, and then killed by Frans, the officer was stripped of his uniform and buried on the spot. They were just in time to cover the hole and hide the uniform in the forest before they were heard and had to flee. The next morning Frans went back early to pick up the uniform and hide it elsewhere so it could be used later as a disguise. Frans then returned to the place where the officer was buried in all haste. There was still a chance that the newly sealed hole would be discovered and excavated, leading to disastrous consequences. Frans broke into the garden shed that belonged to the premises and took a rake. He continued the story: "I raked the path in its entire length to make it seem not too fresh and scattered some moss and twigs over it. After I had finished this, the gardener appeared and discovered me. He got out of bed early, because he was alerted by his dog last night. He started to rant nervously and wanted to report me to the police. I scared him and forced him not to report anything, because then all the work would have been in vain. The forest was always guarded after that and could not be used by me anymore, which was a pity, because I also gave my boys weapon and other military training."[40] Next to one of the ponds in the yard of the "House with the Statues" you could probably still find the remains of this high-ranking German SS officer...

The liquidations the women carried out were fraught with risk. Because there was a constant chance of discovery, Hannie carried her gun in her handbag at all times. Remarkably, before any attack, she always combed her red hair extensively, applied powder to her face and put lipstick on her lips. She did this "to die beautifully," she confided to Truus.[41]

The other important resistance work of the three young women was the housing of Jewish children at safe houses. This was a good job for women because a woman holding a child's hand did not draw much attention. To Truus' great sadness, this did not always end well. One time Truus was on a boat with Jewish children when they were suddenly attacked by Germans. The boat overturned, and the children went into the water. Truus tried to save them, in vain.

Another time, Truus had to take Loetje, a five-year-old boy, to another family. Jewish children often went from one hiding place to another. By means of a coded language, they met each other on the Houtplein and then jumped on their bikes. Truus could tell the child was nervous, so she started singing songs with him while they biked along. Unfortunately, on their ride, they stumbled upon a German column that was unexpectedly shot at by English fighters. Loetje was hit and did not survive.

More often than not, the missions to hide children did go well, but Hannie said she thought this work was so terrible that it only made her cry. She preferred to fight. Only Hannie and Truus could take on this dangerous job. Freddie could not help bring Jewish children to safety because, being the youngest, she still wore her hair in girlish braids and when combined with her dark features, she could be considered a Jewish child and was therefore in danger.[42]

Truus recounted, "A war like this is a very raw experience. While I was biking, I saw Germans picking up innocent people from the streets, putting them against a wall and shooting them. I was forced to watch, which aroused such an enormous anger in me, such a disgust, a feeling of 'dirty bastards.' You can have any political conviction or be totally against war, but at that moment you are just a human being confronted with something very cruel. Shooting innocent people is murder.[43] If you experience something like this, you'll find it justified that when people commit treason, such as exchanging a four-year-old Jewish child for 35 guilders (Dutch currency at that time), you act against it. These are such scary people, who only look at what's in it for them, even if it is a human being.[44]

"Once, I was confronted with an SS soldier, a Dutch SS soldier even, who was killing a small baby by hitting it against a wall. He grabbed the baby and hit it against the wall. The father and sister had to watch. They were obviously hysterical. The child was dead. I shot that guy. Right there and then. That wasn't an assignment, but I don't regret it.[45]

"I really don't regret what we did. You have to see it like this," she continued, "We were dealing with cancerous tumors in society that you had to cut out like a surgeon. You couldn't say, 'Hey, mister, you're doing it wrong,' because then you would risk a bullet through your head, you couldn't arrest him, and you couldn't put him in prison or find a safe house for him because we needed it ourselves for the Jews and people who were in the resistance and had to leave. There was no other solution. That is the cruelty of war. You couldn't try these people at that moment either. You couldn't say, 'Sir, why did you do that? What were your motives?'"[46]

The young women did their work 'Because it had to be done;' they saw it as their duty. Truus continued her account: "What I want to pass on to young people is that if you have to make a decision, that decision must be a right one and you must always remain human."[47]

In addition to Truus and Freddie, Hannie also worked with Jan Bonekamp, a member of the resistance from IJmuiden. Jan was a driver for the Hoogovens blast steel plant in IJmuiden and Hannie admired him. Jan was married and had a daughter but it is thought that Hannie and Jan may have fallen in love with each other during their time together. Some sources even reported they may have had an affair, but those reports later turned out to be unfounded.

One mission that Hannie carried out with Jan Bonekamp, Jan Brasser (commander of the RVV Zaanstreek from Krommenie, whose nickname was "White Ko") and Jan Bak took place on November 24, 1943. They tried to disable the PEN (Provincial Electric Company of North Holland) power plant in Velsen-Noord using explosives. Only part of the cargo exploded, however, damaging just one transport system. The material damage was relatively minor, but the psychological damage of this attack on the population was considerable.[48]

Another act of sabotage took place on January 20, 1944. The RVV attempted to blow up the Rembrandt cinema on the Grote Markt in Haarlem, a cinema that showed propaganda films for the Nazi regime. Pretending to be a couple in love, Hannie Schaft and Cor Rusman attempted to place one firebomb, while Jan Heusdens and Co Kooyman were to place a second firebomb in the theater. The attack failed because the bombs were seen by moviegoers, who warned the Germans. The bombs were disabled in time.[49]

Resistance work was dangerous and required tremendous caution. It was hazardous for women to stay in hiding at the same address for long so they had to move frequently. Truus said, with a sour smile, "I have been in hiding at 51 addresses, I could almost have been Jewish."[50]

One of Truus and Freddie's safe houses was the Corrie ten Boom House of the Ten Boom family at Barteljorisstraat 19. Casper ten Boom owned a watch shop that was located in the same building, called the "Béjé." He lived with his daughters, Betsie (Elisabeth) and Corrie (Cornelia Arnolda Johanna), above the shop. The other children, Willem and Nollie (Arnolda Johanna), no longer lived at home. Nollie ten Boom married Flip (Frederik) van Woerden and together they had six children: Fred (Jacob Frederik), Bob (Casper), Aty (Agatha), Peter (Pieter), Cocky (Cornelia Arnolda) and Els (Elisabeth Johanna). Their house was located at Bosch en Hovenstraat 12, see also the attack on Dicky Wafelbakker further on. Their mother, Cornelia, had died in 1921. In 1943, a secret room was created in Corrie's bedroom, which became a hiding place for Jewish people and resistance fighters.[51]

On February 28, 1944, the SD raided the house while Truus and Freddie were hiding in the same building. At the time of the raid, there was a prayer round (Bible study) going on, so there were quite a few people at the house. Among those present were Casper's daughter, Nollie ten Boom and her son Peter (Pieter) van Woerden. The house was evacuated, and 30 people, including the Ten Boom family, were taken to a prison in Scheveningen "het Oranjehotel." Casper ten Boom died there ten days later.[52]

The house was sealed by the SD; Truus and Freddie, who were still hidden inside, could not get away. They eventually had a chance to escape over the roofs of the adjacent buildings. During their flight, Freddie fell through a glass plate in the roof. Luckily, she landed on a mattress in the mattress shop below at numbers 13–17. Truus and Freddie were forced to spend the night there and went to the next safe house the following day.[53] The four Jewish people still locked up in the building remained hidden in a closet and were finally liberated on March 1, 1944 by two Dutch policemen who were sympathetic to the resistance, Jan Overzet and Theo Ederveen.[54]

According to a statement by Bob van Woerden, one of Nollie ten Boom's sons, his sister Cocky (a friend of Truus) and another person in hiding had the opportunity to return to the watchmaker's via a neighbor's roof just after the raid to bring watches and valuable clocks to safety by hiding them in a pram before the Germans could empty the building.[55]

The SD continued their raids. On March 22, 1944, the pastor of the Catholic Saint Bavo's Cathedral at the Leidschevaart was taken from his bed at night and brought to the Kenaupark. The Germans suspected storage of ammunition in the cathedral. During a search, however, they found only bags of potatoes.[56]

The headquarters of the RVV in Mari Andriessen's house at the Wagenweg was also raided. Mari Andriessen said the following of that raid: "They just walked right in. That infamous police officer Krist was there too. We barely got off the hook, because everywhere in the house were things from the resistance. The laundry basket contained German uniforms, which we used for sabotage. They asked my son what was in the basket. He remained dead calm and said it was dirty laundry. You could just see the guns lying around in my studio, and underneath one of my statues in the yard, there were many grenades. It is incomprehensible that they found nothing."[57] Fortunately, there was no one from the RVV present in the house during the raid, so it was less suspicious. The SD left, but Mari Andriessen was very scared, his family would now be in immediate danger; the RVV had to be creative and meet in various other places.

According to Philine Polak (Hannie's Jewish friend from law school who was in hiding with Hannie's parents) Hannie's parents were proud of their daughter's resistance work, but they were also worried about her. Later, their worries would unfortunately prove to be justified. In an interview, Philine said she once witnessed a conflict between Hannie and her father, who, although Hannie no longer lived at home, wanted to put her under house arrest. Hannie angrily walked out of the house and continued her resistance work with unbridled dedication.[58]

On June 8, 1944, Hannie and Jan Bonekamp attacked the Haarlem confectioner, Piet Faber, a man known for his traitorous practices, often collaborating with his two sons who worked for the SS. Faber had grown suspicious that an attack was being planned against him and had recently fled from his building at the Wagenweg to a rented house at the Jan Tooropkade in Heemstede. He was biking to this house after work when he encountered Hannie and Jan. They attacked him on the corner of Tooropkade-Eerelmanstraat in Heemstede. Faber died a few days later of his injuries in the hospital of the Maria Foundation.[59]

On June 15, 1944, as a response to Faber's killing, an article appeared in the German-controlled *Haarlemsche Courant*:

"Savagery:"

May the cowardice of the murder of a defenseless man be brought to light and horrified at the thought that it is here a woman who is guilty of transgressing the life, the life to the production of which God calls the woman.[60]

It is striking that the emphasis here is on the perpetrator's gender, on the fact that Hannie—as the perpetrator—was a woman. A liquidation was always condemned by the Germans, but now all the more so.

On June 12, 1944, Hannie and Jan Bonekamp began to prepare an attack on the Zaandam police officer Ragut. Ragut worked at the "Sicherheits Polizei" (SP, or Security Police) Amsterdam. On that same day, a number of fellow resistance members were executed after a robbery at the Weteringschans in Amsterdam. Among them was Gerrit van der Veen, an important person within the resistance who had, among other things, attacked the Amsterdam population register. Because the German occupiers could easily track down people through the well-organized official population register, Gerrit van der Veen had set fire to this register on March 27, 1943. Only part of it was destroyed and there was a second copy at the administration in the political capital The Hague, 35 miles south-west of Haarlem, but it was still regarded as an important act of resistance. Hannie and Jan were deeply devastated; Van der Veen's death made them even more determined in their work. [61]

On the evening of June 21, 1944, Hannie came to Truus very upset. In between her tears, she said that something had gone completely wrong and that Jan Bonekamp had been caught. Truus gave her a glass of water to try to calm her nerves, but Hannie's shaking hands knocked all the water over the edge of the glass.[62] Hannie and Jan Bonekamp had been ordered by Jan Brasser to liquidate Ragut earlier that day.

Jan Bonekamp was in hiding with Jan and Trijntje Bult at Pagenlaan 8 in Limmen and Hannie had been in hiding there for the past month as well. Early that morning, Hannie and Jan left Jan and Trijntje Bult's house on bicycles and waited for Ragut in Zaandam. At one point, they saw him cycling on the Westzijde in Zaandam. He was known to often carry two guns on him, so they had to be very careful.[63]

What happened next is unclear. According to Ton Kors' book, "Hannie Schaft. Het levensverhaal van een vrouw in verzet tegen de nazi's," Hannie was the first to fire a shot, as agreed, and kept biking. When Jan fired a second shot, Ragut returned fire and Jan was hit in the abdomen.[64] However, according to Frans van der Wiel's statement, it was Jan who was the first to shoot. Ragut seemed to be dead, so Jan biked on; when Hannie arrived, she saw Ragut pull himself up with his last bit of strength and shoot Jan in the back. Jan then fled and Hannie biked away for her own safety.[65]

Hannie came crying to Truus that evening, full of self-reproach because she felt so bad that Jan had been shot and that she had not gone back to help him. Truus promised her that they would see what they could do the next day.

A day later Hannie and Truus went to the Wilhelmina Hospital in Amsterdam. While they were at the hospital, they heard sirens. An ambulance arrived and two armed SS officers and two nurses carried a stretcher inside. On the stretcher was a severely injured man with a bunch of curls protruding above the blankets. Hannie whispered, "Oh Jan, Jan."[66]

Realizing there was nothing they could do, Truus brought the dejected and sick (she would later be diagnosed with the mumps) Hannie to Frans van der Wiel. On the way, they were stopped by the Germans. Fortunately, Hannie was wearing a headscarf to cover her infamous red hair. The two young women were carrying their FN guns in their pockets, but the guns were not discovered and they were allowed to pass.

Only later did they hear what had happened to Jan. He had been hit in his abdomen and spine. When he had knocked on a door and asked the two old women who answered for help, they had warned the police, who in turn had warned the SD. Shortly after arriving at the hospital, Jan became blind and died soon after. What happened just before his death is not clear. It is believed that a nurse who pretended to be a member of the resistance asked Jan if she could do anything for him. Jan would have mentioned Hannie's name and address at the Van Dortstraat.[67] According to Frans van der Wiel, Jan may have had a photo and the address of Hannie in his pocket.[68]

The RVV ordered Hannie to go into hiding immediately. She went to stay with one of her father's colleagues, Harm Elsinga. Her friend, Philine Polak, who was still in hiding at the Van Dortstraat, also left for a new address. A week later the SP, led by Emil Rühl, raided the Van Dortstraat. Hannie's parents were taken hostage and sent to the Vught concentration camp located near the city of 's-Hertogenbosch in the southern part of the Netherlands. The Germans hoped that Hannie would turn herself in. Even Hitler seemed to have demanded to track her down.[69]

Freddie and Truus Oversteegen at Evacuation Hospital Twente
in 1943. (Courtesy of North Holland Archives)

Truus and Freddie Oversteegen at Evacuation Hospital Twente
in 1943. (Courtesy of North Holland Archives)

Bombardment at Amsterdamse buurt in Haarlem,
April 16, 1943. (Courtesy of North Holland Archives)

Headquarters of the RVV and home of Mari Andriessen, 2018.
(Photo by Sophie Poldermans)

"House with the Statues," 1944. (Photo by Hans Poldermans)

"House with the Statues," 2018. (Photo by Sophie Poldermans)

Backyard of "House with the Statues," 2018. (Photo by Sophie Poldermans)

Haarlemmerhout, 2018. (Photo by Sophie Poldermans)

Truus Oversteegen with Sten gun, 1945.
(Courtesy of North Holland Archives)

Hannie Schaft's 9-mm FN 28730 gun, 2018. (Photo by Sophie
Poldermans, collection of North Holland Archives)

Jan Bonekamp, n.d. (Courtesy of North Holland Archives)

Jan Heusdens, April 9, 2010. (Photo by Maarten Poldermans)

Concentration camp Vught, 2018, where Hannie Schaft's parents
were held hostage. (Photo by Sophie Poldermans)

Paul Elsinga at Mari Andriessen's house, April 22, 2013.
(Courtesy of National Hannie Schaft Foundation)

Buitenrustlaan 22, 2018: house of Elsinga family and safe house of Hannie
Schaft and Truus Oversteegen. (Photo by Sophie Poldermans)

Chapter 6

The Resistance Work Grew More Perilous

J AN BONEKAMP'S DEATH WAS A HEAVY BLOW FOR HANNIE. Truus talked to her for hours on end, in vain; Hannie was inconsolable. The whole country was in a festive mood after "D-day" (the successful landing of the Allies in Normandy on June 6, 1944), but Hannie was by no means in a festive mood. She was anxious and depressed.

Hannie had to be even more careful now. She dyed her red hair black and straightened it. She also borrowed glasses made with window glass from Erna Kropveld to further disguise herself. Fortunately, a few months earlier, on March 8, 1944, she had received a completely new identification card in the population register via a reliable official in the town hall in Velsen. It was issued in the name of Johanna Elderkamp, a woman who was born in Zurich, Switzerland. It was an identity the Germans could not check.[70]

Hannie even played with the idea of turning herself in. Truus and Freddie managed to talk her out of that but with great difficulty. Truus and Freddie told Hannie that the Germans would never let her parents go if she turned herself in. After a while, Hannie's parents were released due to the lack of information about the possible whereabouts of their daughter. Luckily, Hannie had never told her parents anything.

Hannie found some peace with the Elsinga family. Harm Elsinga was the principal of the Rijksleerschool at Schreveliusstraat 27 and lived with his wife Lien and their two sons, Ruud and Paul, at the Buitenrustlaan 22. Hannie stayed there and used the nick name Eva or Hannie de Wit.[71]

The youngest son of the family, Paul Elsinga (b. November 24, 1933), was ten years old at the time. He remembers Hannie was hiding with them. Paul said about that time, "Hannie was always very friendly. She was very sweet to me. For example, she helped me with my homework."[72] All kinds of people from the resistance came to their house. Although Paul was very young, his parents had told him what was happening at their home. He was explicitly instructed to keep quiet about it.

Harm Elsinga had several items at his school that were used for the resistance. Occasionally, he sent Paul on errands under the guise of innocent neighborhood deliveries. For example, after school Paul was sometimes given a school bag that he was instructed to hand over to certain people from the resistance. He had to learn the addresses by heart and hand over the bag under a code name. Usually, the bag contained illegal journals, but sometimes the bag was heavier and probably contained ammunition. He could be easily deployed, since a child with a school bag was in no way suspicious.[73]

Truus also lived with the Elsinga family, along with Hannie, in their attic for a time. Paul remembers an incident when his parents were not home. He came home from school in the afternoon with Truus, and when she searched in her bag for the key to open the door, her gun fell out into the street. Paul gaped at her in astonishment with big eyes, and Truus said to him, "I am a soldier of Prince Bernhard. If you do not talk to anyone about this, you are too." It was only after the war that Paul dared to tell his parents. According to Paul, Truus was usually very precise when it came to things like that. "Hannie was much more careless; she had ammunition lying around the house, sometimes even whole cartridge holders. My father often had to scold her so she would be more careful."[74]

On July 30, 1944, the "Terror-und-Sabotage-Erlass" was issued, in which Hitler changed and tightened the rules regarding the treatment of opponents of the Nazi regime. One new rule said that armed opponents were to be shot on the spot.[75]

Slowly but surely Hannie began to do resistance work again. In a letter from Hannie to Philine on September 4, 1944, a clear picture emerges of a sad, somewhat bitter and emotional woman. However, the letter also contains rational elements emphasizing the importance of intellect and looking at how one can serve to rebuild society. Finally, there is also hope in the letter, since Hannie dares to look ahead, to the future, to a time after the war, although she does not know exactly when that will be. The letter reads as follows:

"Dear Philine,

Since my pen still leaks, I will write with pencil. I've just washed my hands. The fact that you haven't heard from me for so long isn't my fault: the previous letter (from 2 weeks ago) had to be torn apart at some point. I really like it that you're doing so well. This could have been different, very different! I'm in the very best of health. Since a few weeks I am back in function, just in time, otherwise I would have gone mad. I'm in a very sad spiritual state: I can't read a book, a novel, or a study book. In my spare time I knit socks! Does that sound familiar to you? I am considerably less tough than I thought: being confronted with death was not easy. And in this case, it was very direct. Unemployment since then has not exactly calmed me down either. And now it's too late. I will still try to save the debris from my old self. But that probably isn't possible anymore. People are in such a party mood. I'm there like a smiling Buddha and they expect me to be in a party mood too. I would rather swear. Unfortunately, I can only do that with you and a few other people. When the war is over, and you're crying in a corner, I will come to you to do this activity. Dear child, I would like to come to you, but you understand that I cannot leave at the moment. So, it will have to be "after the war." When will that be? Maybe on my birthday. Now I'm becoming melodramatic: if I don't see you at all anymore, I will give you some guidelines for the future a. Solidarity b. Continuation of all our work. We are just a two-unity, and intellect is desperately needed for our cause, and our social conversion (or demolition—construction) c. Don't think anything cowardly of my friend. He behaved beautifully. You would hope there would be more people like him. He was one of the finest guys I ever met. Remember this, it is very important. Philine, see you soon.

Warm regards,

Jo.

P.S. I catch fleas almost every day!"[76]

On Tuesday September 5, 1944, Radio Oranje reported that the Allies were near Breda, in the southern part of the Netherlands. Many people celebrated on the streets, while people in hiding showed themselves openly on the streets. Germans and NSB soldiers fled en masse, even the Haarlem NSB Mayor Plekker fled. Alas, this report turned out to be false. The excitement about a possible liberation was premature and the day became known as "Mad Tuesday." Instead of Canadian liberators, the people saw the German occupiers at the Wagenweg again.[77]

Shortly after "Mad Tuesday," a decision was announced that the various resistance organizations needed to cooperate. An umbrella body, the Internal Armed Forces (BS), headed by Prince Bernhard, was created. During this time, a number of people still joined the resistance. These people were called "September flies."

Truus later revealed the following about the resistance work: "We only fought against *real* fascists, not against innocent people. For example, we refused the kidnapping of Seyss-Inquart's children, the Commissioner of the Reich of the Netherlands." Freddie was the fiercest and immediately refused to involve children in the fight. Truus and Hannie agreed. Hannie said the following about her work in the resistance: "We are not Hitlerians; resistance fighters do not kill children."[78] Children should never be the victims of any action. Hannie, Truus and Freddie were very adamant about that.

In the month following "Mad Tuesday" events began to intensify. On September 11, Hitler introduced an even stricter measure: all resistance fighters were to be shot ruthlessly, even if they did not carry any weapons.[79]

On September 17, large-scale Allied airborne landings took place in Arnhem and Nijmegen in the eastern part of the Netherlands as part of Operation Market Garden. British general Montgomery wanted to gain control over important bridges in the east of the country in order to move into neighboring Germany. This would also make it possible for Allied Forces to surround the German army in the western part of the Netherlands. Some operations were successful. Nevertheless, the German army beat back and the Battle of Arnhem was lost. It appeared to be "a bridge too far" as British lieutenant general Browning had warned general Montgomery. Operation Market Garden had failed. Notwithstanding, the Allied troops did reach Nijmegen. In the weeks that followed, several parts of the southern part of the Netherlands were liberated. After that, it remained quiet on the battleground. In Haarlem, the Allied landings in Arnhem caused more NSB officials to flee. However, the western and northern parts of the Netherlands would still await a long and cold winter.

Prime Minister of the Netherlands Gerbrandy called, from the government in exile in London, for a general railway strike to support the Allied operations. The Germans then claimed all means of transport, which seriously stagnated all transportation. This led to major food shortages in the west, which would later result in the Dutch famine of 1944–1945, known as the "Hunger Winter."

The Germans became more aggressive and tightened their checkpoints, even starting to confiscate bicycles on a large scale. In Haarlem-Noord, the residents had to evacuate, which meant the people in hiding were forced to find a new place to go. Evacuation plans were also prepared for IJmuiden, Bloemendaal, Santpoort, Driehuis and Beverwijk so that the Germans could better defend their access to the North Sea Canal in case of a possible Allied invasion.[80]

On September 22, only two hours of gas per day were delivered to the residents of Haarlem, and on October 9, the electricity supply was cut off. As the Germans tightened their grip on the region, the resistance escalated their actions.[81]

The RVV had already been preparing to liquidate the leaders of the Haarlem criminal investigation service: inspector Fake Krist and his subordinates, Willemse and Smit. Independent of the RVV, other resistance groups were also targeting these three men.

Jan Heusdens and Truus attacked Smit at the Spaarndamseweg on September 5, 1944. This attack failed, and Jan got a bullet in his leg. The attack on Fake Krist also failed.[82]

On the same day, Willemse was attacked by Hannie and Cor Rusman at Schoterweg. Hannie hit Willemse in his arm, but then her gun failed. As she tried to fix her gun, she fell. Willemse moved toward her and shot her, one bullet going through her thigh. Cor took Hannie to her parents' general practitioner, the trustworthy doctor Lancée at the Duinoordstraat. Hannie was lucky: the bullet had gone straight through the flesh of her leg, without hitting any major structures. Again, she had to go into hiding, this time with a teacher, W. ter Horst, at the Ramplaan. She stayed there for a week, after which she went back to the Elsinga family.[83]

After the invasion of Mari Andriessen's house, the RVV no longer had fixed headquarters. Meetings always took place in different locations. One of these meeting places was a houseboat in the Leidschevaart on the border of Haarlem and Heemstede.[84]

On October 25, 1944, Hannie and Truus were in the neighborhood of the Catholic Saint Bavo's Cathedral at the Leidschevaart at half past seven in the morning. They planned to attack Fake Krist again. After four previous attempts by various resistance groups, they hoped to finally be successful in liquidating him. At a quarter past eight, they saw him approaching on a bicycle along the Westergracht, but just when Hannie and Truus were about to bike toward him, they heard five shots.

Paul Elsinga also heard these shots. He was with his father in the classroom so the family could stay close together during these times. The Rijksleerschool (elementary school, now the "international school") at Schreveliusstraat 27 and the Rijkskweekschool for the training of elementary school teachers (now a branch of the First Christian Lyceum) at Leidschevaart 220 were in the same building (with two entrances) within hearing distance of the site of the attack on Fake Krist. Upon hearing these shots, Harm Elsinga winked at his son Paul, knowing that an attack on Fake Krist by Hannie and Truus was about to happen and thinking that they were the ones who had fired the shots.[85]

All shots hit the target. Fake Krist fell dead from his bike. Another resistance group had been ahead of them. It was pure coincidence that two resistance groups had planned an attack not only on the same day but also at the same time. "Black Kees," or Gommert Krijger, had shot from the school at the corner of Westergracht-Leidschevaart. Hannie and Truus told the people around them that they would warn the police and then quickly biked away. The other resistance group that had fired shots from the school also escaped the Germans just in time.[86] To this day, the bullet holes are still present in the wall of the Catholic Saint Bavo's Cathedral.

Paul Elsinga remembers just after the liquidation of Fake Krist, a German soldier with a drawn pistol entered his classroom, a moment that made a deep impression on him. The Rijksleerschool was just on the border of the area that the Germans wanted to occupy. The soldier wanted to have keys to everything so that the Germans could reach the building and the surrounding area via both the Leidschevaart and the Schreveliusstraat.[87]

In retaliation for the liquidation of Fake Krist, eight houses on the corner of Leidsezijstraat-Westergracht had to be vacated the next day, October 26, after which they were set on fire. A little later, ten hostages were taken and shot. Truus was at this site, she had gone there to see how the liquidation had been committed. With others, she was arrested when she walked by and was forced to watch the Germans take their revenge. When the Germans put the guns to their shoulders, an elderly man, who was one of the hostages, hesitantly began to sing the "Wilhelmus" (the Dutch national anthem). Shots sounded and then it was quiet.[88]

During the Hunger Winter there was a great shortage of food and fuel. It is estimated that some 20,000 people died from malnutrition and cold. People literally ate everything they could find. At the time, Hannie and Truus were hiding with Ms. Schakel-Braakensiek on the corner of the Dr. P. Cuyperslaan and the Hendrik de Keyserlaan in Heemstede. Ms. Schakel-Braakensiek, who had lived in the Dutch East Indies for a long time, managed to turn tulip bulbs into a somewhat edible Indonesian meal.[89]

Paul Elsinga also remembers the cold winter well. He only went to school for one hour a day because there was no heat in the school buildings and the children had to wear their coats in the classroom. There was only time for short explanations, and then the children went home again. Some children could not go to school at all because they simply did not have any clothes to wear to protect them from the cold—a very poignant situation.[90]

At that time, Hannie and Truus expanded their contacts with other resistance groups in Haarlem and its surrounding areas for the RVV. Not all resistance groups were as good as they were, however. Hannie and Truus found this out the hard way. They were often asked to take parcels for members of the Velsen resistance, but when they noticed that they were being used to deliver insignificant items and were being deliberately exposed to major risks, they immediately refused to provide these services any longer. After the war, it was revealed that this resistance group had played a double role. This was called the "Velsen Affair" and became a national scandal after liberation.[91]

The winter of 1944-1945 was difficult for Hannie, Truus and Freddie who suffered from hunger along with their countrymen. Moreover, Hannie was still struggling with a certain degree of despondency and despair that arose after the death of Jan Bonekamp. Hannie's fellow student, Annie van Calsem, remembered that Hannie had been at Annie's parents' doorstep for shelter during the Hunger Winter. Annie had this to say about Hannie during that time: "Hannie was nervous, skinny, overtired, hunted, her hands were shaking, she dressed poorly, the black dye of her hair was disappearing, revealing the copper color." In short, she was not feeling well.[92]

Truus and Freddie now started talking about the future and making plans more often, but Hannie did not participate. She once remarked that she thought she would not experience the end of the war. For her it was as if a large curtain had dropped. She once said, "I might even be buried in a coffin covered with the tricolor (the Dutch flag is red, white and blue) and the Queen would be present."[93]

The suffering of the Hunger Winter did not slow the women down, on the contrary. At the end of 1944 or the beginning of 1945, Hannie and Truus tried to blow up the railway bridge over the Spaarne river to prevent the Germans from transporting company installations of the Hoogovens to Germany by train. The attack failed; however, they did succeed in blowing up part of the railway from IJmuiden to Velsen, in the Netelbos. As a result, rail traffic was down for weeks.[94]

During the last months before the end of the war, Hannie, Truus and Freddie also had frequent contact with a small Roman Catholic resistance group from IJmuiden-Oost. The three leaders of this group were Father Pontianus, Coen Hamers Sr. and Mr. Marcelis. Their main activities consisted of exploring the coastal area and forging papers (including port "Ausweisen" or IDs), and using false German service stamps in order to gain access to the dunes to monitor the construction and reinforcement of the "Atlantic Wall." Others made maps of the construction, which were forwarded to the government in London. IJmuiden, also known as "Festung IJmuiden" (Fortress IJmuiden), was more or less closed. There were now only two crossing points: one near the Duin en Kruidbergerweg, where cemetery Westerveld is now located, and one where the Tunnelweg is now located. Ration coupons were also falsified. To organize this activity, they had contact with groups from Santpoort, Bloemendaal and Haarlem.[95]

Coen Hamers Sr. was engaged to Jo Post, who was also part of this resistance group, and did a lot of courier work. Jo's father, Cees (Cornelis) Post, was the one who organized meetings for the various local resistance groups at his home. The Heerenduinweg 56 in IJmuiden was also known under the pseudonym "Commando Post," after the initials of Cees Post (CP). The Commando Post had facilitated contact between the resistance group IJmuiden-Oost and Jan Bonekamp, and through him with the resistance trio, Hannie, Truus and Freddie. Truus and Freddie also stayed at the Commando Post several times. Piet Menger, later Truus' husband, was also a member of the IJmuiden-Oost group.[96]

At one point, Jo Post was commissioned by the resistance to do courier work and to deliver a list of addresses of resistance members of the IJmuiden-Oost group to an address in Bloemendaal for Mr. Sikkel, district attorney in Haarlem and Regional Commander of the Internal Armed Forces. An unknown person (some believe it to have been Mr. Sikkel) betrayed the resistance. Using the information Jo Post had unwittingly provided, the Germans attacked eight houses belonging to members of the resistance. A few were able to escape just in time, but several others were taken prisoner at the Weteringschans in Amsterdam, and one was even shot. Just prior to this set of raids, the Germans had sent soldiers to the home of twin brothers, Hein (Henricus Gerardus) and Nol (Arnoldus Johannes) van Broekhuysen, at the Lijsterlaan 4. Nol was blamed for making the illegal drawings of the defense works and was, therefore, to be executed by the Germans. Because of a misunderstanding and a mix-up, not Nol but his twin brother Hein was executed. Nol's fiancée, Suus de Jager, had red hair. At first, the Germans thought she was the famous girl with the red hair, Hannie Schaft. Fortunately for Suus, Hannie Schaft was captured not that much later, and her arrest probably saved Suus' life.[97] On the same day a resistance group was arrested in Haarlem-Noord and all of its members were executed.

While the Germans were arresting and executing resistance fighters, Mr. Sikkel ordered the assassination of one of their own: Ko de Kruijff, a resistance man who had become too talkative. Gommert Krijger's (or "Black Kees'") assault group carried out the deed in his cell in a police station in Heemstede. Several people, including Mr. Sikkel, played dubious roles in this assault. This is probably related to the aforementioned "Velsen Affair."[98] The traitor was never revealed.

On March 1, 1945, Hannie and Truus disguised themselves as workmen, and liquidated Willem Zirkzee, a collaborating NSB police inspector who worked closely together with the SD in Amsterdam. This attack was ordered by Mr. Sikkel, and executed close to Zirkzee's home at the Leidschevaart 18–22, where the Krelagehuis used to be. Two days later, as a reprisal, 15 men were taken from prison at the Weteringschans in Amsterdam and were shot at the Dreef in Haarlem while a crowd of people was forced to watch. Immediately after liberation, a temporary monument was erected on this spot on the Dreef and after the war, on March 7, 1949 the statue "Man in Front of the Firing Squad" created by Mari Andriessen, was unveiled.[99]

On March 15, 1945, Hannie and Truus attacked Ko Langendijk, a men's hairdresser in IJmuiden and Velsen-Noord at the Staten Bolwerk. Ko had given information to the SD for money and later joined the Velsen police force as an SS officer. Hannie and Truus arrived together on bikes. Hannie shot first, but her gun failed. Truus then tried to kill him, but despite hitting Langendijk in his head and his back, he survived. His fiancée, who was standing next to him, began to scream. Then the "Feldgendarmerie" (military police) arrived.[100]

Truus and Hannie had to escape. They fled to Café Spoorzicht, despite knowing the tenant could not be trusted. Truus pulled out her gun and shouted, "Gentlemen, your attention please, we're coming in now, but when the Germans come in, we've been here all afternoon. If you do not behave the way we want you to, and we're on our way to heaven, we will take a few of you with us. We do not intend to just give up." They ordered a drink to make their breath smell of alcohol and pretended to be drunk. When a high-ranking German soldier came in, Truus hung around his neck and shouted, "Ha Heinz, come here." Her behavior was annoying and vulgar to the soldier that he left. Truus recalled with a sigh, "Well, you had to play that role too…"[101]

Truus explained that carrying out these attacks was not easy on a person. Hannie and Freddie were always extremely nervous before their missions. In fact, Freddie would get so nervous that she would almost eat her handkerchief. Truus did not suffer from anxiety at the moment of the attacks, but afterward she would faint or become overwhelmed and have a heavy crying fit.[102]

On March 19, 1945, Truus and Hannie liquidated Gerdo Bakker in the Schoterstraat in Haarlem. Gerdo Bakker had a lot of money he obtained from workers of the German "Wehrmacht" (German army). This assignment came from the Velsen resistance.[103]

On March 21, 1945, Hannie and Truus attacked Madame Sieval (sometimes written as Cheval), probably a lady of French descent. According to the RVV, she had betrayed local residents and had reported them to the SD and the Haarlem police chief, Fake Krist. For days leading up to their attack, Freddie would search the neighborhood, and Truus and Hannie would hide indoors with reliable people at the Twijnderslaan, where Madame Sieval lived at number 46. The resistance trio came up with all sorts of ideas on how to carry out the attack, but Madame Sieval almost never went outside.

Their first two attempts failed. The first time Madame Sieval finally went outside, she had a little boy by her side on a sled, who turned out to be her four-year-old son. That went too far for Hannie, Truus and Freddie. They resolutely refused to commit an attack involving a child.

The second failed attack occurred when Hannie, Truus and Freddie saw Madame Sieval at the corner of Twijnderslaan-Kleine Houtweg. Hannie shot first, and Truus followed. Madame Sieval started screaming. Freddie acted as the lookout and warned that a group of children and a number of Germans were arriving. Truus shot once more and they escaped as quickly as possible. Later it turned out that Madame Sieval had been very lucky. Although a number of bullets had been fired at her from fairly close range, she had been only slightly injured. Her thick fur coat had caught the bullets.[104]

In the last weeks before the liberation, the Internal Armed Forces and the occupying forces agreed that the resistance would refrain from liquidations and that the Germans in turn would not execute any more prisoners. However, neither party actually complied with the agreement.[105]

Truus and Freddie's next target was Dicky (Gerbranda Margaretha) Wafelbakker in the Bosch and Hovenstraat. Dicky was a journalist at the *Haarlems Dagblad* and a translator of English detective stories, who lived at the Bosch and Hovenstraat 4. It was widely known that she had betrayed people from her own street and had reported them to the SD in the Kenaupark.

One of the people she had betrayed was the aforementioned Bob (Casper) van Woerden. His parents' home, named "Frecasaty" after the three oldest children, was located at Bosch and Hovenstraat 12. Bob's mother Nollie ten Boom received regular visits from her sister, Corrie ten Boom. Corrie described these visits in her book, *The Hiding Place*.[106] Nollie's husband, Flip van Woerden, was also known in the neighborhood as the principal of the elementary school, the Dreefschool, in Haarlem.

Bob was a member of a resistance group in Haarlem-Zuid and was hiding in the Wilhelminapark with Ms. Bühning because of his resistance activities.

In a testimony, Bob recounted that one day he was visiting a friend in the resistance, Dick Hoorens van Heyningen. Dick lived together with his mother, Julia Giesberts, at Bosch and Hovenstraat 4, just a few doors down from Nollie and Flip's house. At the same address, Dicky Wafelbakker was renting a room from Ms. Giesberts.

During his visit, Bob had told Dick about his resistance work and had explained where he was hiding. The houses in the Bosch and Hovenstraat were old and poorly insulated, and the walls were thin. Dicky Wafelbakker's room was adjacent to that of Dick. Probably because of this, Dicky had heard where Bob van Woerden was hiding and had passed on this information.[107]

A few days later, Bob received a message that his safe house was known to the SD and that he had to move to another address as soon as possible. During Dicky's absence, Bob searched her room together with Dick Hoorens van Heyningen and found that she had his personal details, exactly as he had passed them on. He reported this immediately to the RVV.[108]

Other sources reported that a letter from Dicky Wafelbakker, in which nine people had been betrayed, including Bob van Woerden, had been intercepted by a postman sympathetic to the resistance. The RVV was immediately notified.[109]

On April 13, 1945, Dicky Wafelbakker walked back from the soup kitchen in the depot of the North-South-Holland Tramway Society (NZHTM) at the Leidschevaart. Meanwhile, Truus rode her bike, with Freddie sitting on the back, from the Vredenhofstraat and turned right into the Bosch and Hovenstraat. Truus got off her bike and walked beside it with Freddie right behind her. They approached Dicky and asked her if she was indeed Dicky Wafelbakker. After Dicky confirmed that she was, Truus immediately shot her. Dicky Wafelbakker fell dead, with the soup kitchen pan still in her hand. At that moment, Bob van Woerden was in his parents' home at number 12. He was standing in front of the open window on the first floor and witnessed the liquidation.[110]

Remarkably, Kees Schipper, a 14-year-old boy and a former student of the Dreefschool, living with his grandmother and mother at number 17, also witnessed the liquidation. Kees had occasionally done small jobs for the resistance. In an extensive statement, he described that he had also just come back from the soup kitchen and had heard two or three loud blasts that caused him to rush home without investigating. A little while later he grew curious about what had happened and joined the group of people gathered around the body of Dicky on the street in front of number 14. Dicky lay on her back, her legs half under her body, with her arms spread. Doctor Westra, an anthroposophical doctor at the Oranjeplein, asked if he could examine her; he noticed that the number of shots in Dicky's chest had proved fatal.[111]

Kees Schipper had picked up a bullet case from the street and put it in his pocket. His neighbor Els had seen him pick up the bullet case and asked him to hand it over to her. "Far too dangerous," she said and threw the case into the sewer drain.[112] The neighbor Els whom Kees mentioned in his statement was probably Els van Woerden, who lived at number 12. That house was diagonally opposite Kees' house at number 17, and Els was the same age as Kees at the time.

According to Kees, Ms. Kaplan, who lived at number 2, had asked Truus and Freddie as they quickly tried to get away on their bikes, "Why are you doing that?" to which Freddie probably replied, "Spy!" Kees suffered emotionally from this attack and cried in his bed that evening.[113]

Freddie later stated that she thought it was different to shoot a woman than a man.[114]

For a long time, it was unclear who was responsible for the liquidation of Dicky Wafelbakker. Truus wrote in a letter that it was her and her sister Freddie who had carried out this liquidation by order of the resistance.[115]

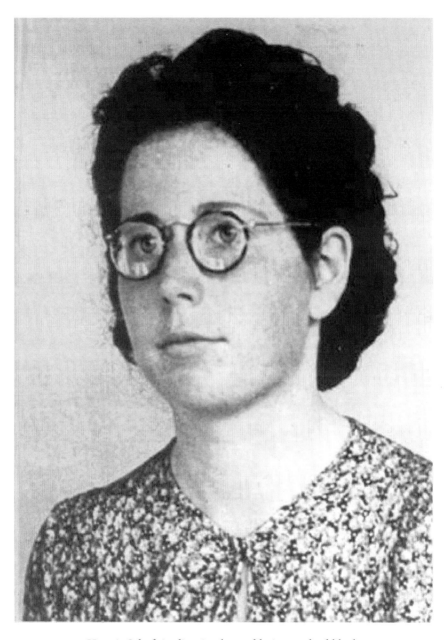

Hannie Schaft in disguise: her red hair was dyed black,
and she is wearing glasses made of window glass, n.d.
(Photo by Harm Elsinga, Courtesy of North Holland Archives)

Truus Oversteegen and Hannie Schaft in disguise, with Truus Oversteegen dressed up as a man at Dentist Grouwstra in Iordensstraat, Haarlem, 1945. (Courtesy of North Holland Archives)

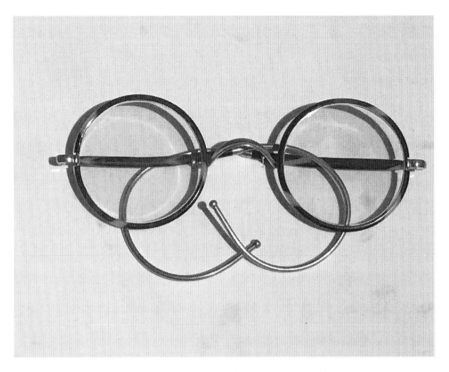

Glasses used by Hannie Schaft to disguise herself, 2018.
(Photo by Sophie Poldermans, collection of Resistance Museum Amsterdam)

Liquidation of Fake Krist at Westergracht on October 25,
1944. (Courtesy of North Holland Archives)

Statue, "Grieving woman," 2018, where ten hostages were killed after the
liquidation of Fake Krist at Westergracht on October 26, 1944. The Catholic Saint
Bavo's Cathedral shows in the background. (Photo by Sophie Poldermans)

Haarlemmerhout, chopping wood for stoves,
Hunger Winter 1944. (Photo by Hans Poldermans)

Jo Hamers-Post (at age 84) and Coen Hamers Sr. (at age 86), backyard of their home in Velsen-Zuid, 2005. (Courtesy of Coen Hamers Jr.)

Piet Menger, n.d. (Courtesy of North Holland Archives)

Chapter 7

The Arrest and Execution of Hannie Schaft

PEOPLE FELT THE JOY OF LIBERATION IN MARCH OF 1945. Swedish bread and margarine, which were brought in by barge from Delfzijl in the far north of the country, were regularly distributed in the starving Randstad (a megalopolis in the central/western part of the Netherlands, consisting of the four largest cities of the country: Amsterdam, Rotterdam, The Hague and Utrecht).

On March 21, 1945, the same day as the failed attack on Madame Sieval, Hannie left early in the evening from her safe house at the Elsingas to IJmuiden to deliver a pack of *Waarheid* ("Truth") and *Vrij Nederland* newspapers and to map the defenses. She would not sleep at home that night.

In Haarlem-Noord, she was arrested during a routine check at the Jan Gijzenbrug at the Rijksstraatweg. The Germans had constructed a heavy concrete roadblock, which was popularly referred to with the German and Dutch word for wall: the "Mauer-muur." Hannie's arrest took place in a narrow passage in this wall.

At a check point in the wall, Hannie was stopped and forced to open her pannier bags attached to her bike for inspection. While digging through her bags, the two inspecting German soldiers stumbled upon the resistance newspapers. Her handbag (the German soldiers did not know that Hannie's handbag contained her gun, a 9-mm FN 28730) was also taken from her.[116]

She recognized the commanding officer with the two soldiers, Lieutenant Willy Lages, with whom she had talked a few years earlier in the Stoops swimming pool in Overveen. She called his name, but he pretended to not know her and stayed at a distance. Meanwhile, Commander Frans van der Wiel's two sisters had seen Hannie standing at the "Mauer-muur." They tried to reach their brothers Frans and Sander and also Truus and Freddie, but they did not succeed. Hannie was taken by car to the Ripperdakazerne at the Kleverlaan for interrogation.

From the Ripperdakazerne, she was transferred to German headquarters, the Ortskommandantur, in the Haarlemmerhout. The headquarters were located in Hotel Den Hout at the Fonteinlaan, next to the current restaurant Dreefzicht, where she was also interrogated. Hannie did not say a word. At the end of the evening, she was taken to the Haarlem House of Detention the "Koepel," at the Oostvest. Only there did the Germans check Hannie's handbag and discover her gun. Hannie was taken to cell 18 on the first floor. A special sentry had to ensure that nobody could come into contact with the prisoner. Two Dutchmen, Haverkort and Bijl, worked the shifts one after the other. The latter looked for a way to get Hannie out of prison that same evening, but he failed to do so. That evening, Hannie was taken from her cell by German Emil Rühl, who happened to be in the Haarlem House of Detention, and she was taken to the Amsterdam House of Detention at the Amstelveenseweg.[117]

At Halfweg, Rühl found out their captive was the girl with the red hair who was sought after fiercely. Rühl was charged with the investigation and

Hannie was intensively questioned at the Amstelveenseweg. The SD top executive, Willy Lages, was informed of her arrest, as were the SD officers Viermann and Viebahn. Hannie was alone in her cell, isolated from others. On her door hung a sign: "Mörderin" (Murderer). She was made to wash the black out of her hair so it turned red again. The Germans now knew for sure that she was Hannie Schaft, "das Rothaarige Mädel" (the girl with the red hair), whom they had been looking for for so long.[118]

Ada van Rossem, a female doctor who was also imprisoned at the Amstelveenseweg for having had an illegal radio station in her house, said in a testimony, "I have seen her. I stood at the top of the gallery and saw that she was being taken to her cell. She was downstairs, isolated. She was wearing a sweater and a skirt. I think she was at the end of her tether." Ada had heard from the guards that Hannie was acting very strangely—she did not want to wash herself, eat or put her slop bucket outside anymore.

Although Hannie was questioned day and night and was even tortured, she did not divulge any names. The Elsingas were raided by Willy Lages (SD), Emil Rühl (SP) and Ferdinand Aus der Fünten (SS "Hauptsturmführer," a mid-level commander).[119] Ton Kors' book mentioned a fourth German who was present at that raid as well. The Germans knew that Hannie hid at the Elsinga's house before her arrest because of her officially registered forged identity card. Paul Elsinga said this about the raid: "One morning we had a raid from the Germans. My mother and I were home; my father and older brother were not. They turned Hannie's room upside down. They took a lot of clothes and other stuff. There was a baby picture of Paul's older brother on the wall of Hannie's room. A German stood looking at it and said, "Dicker Kopf" (fat face), whereupon Paul's mother responded, "We still had food then." Paul added in his account of the raid, "That's right. My mother could be fierce."[120] Then the Elsingas were left alone.

Ko Langendijk's fiancée recognized Hannie and pointed her out in prison as the perpetrator of the earlier attack on Ko Langendijk at the Staten

Bolwerk. Eventually, Hannie admitted to the attack and as a result, five women who were supposed to be executed as a reprisal for Ko Langendijk's attack were spared execution. Hannie also admitted to the attacks on Ragut, Faber, Smit and Willemse.[121]

Hannie was photographed in the courtyard of the House of Detention. The police photos show Hannie, who probably thought she would be executed, with teary eyes and tightly clenched fists, a handkerchief sandwiched into the band of her skirt.

Freddie was also stopped by the Germans on the same day as Hannie. She had left the house with her gun (despite the fact that the RVV forbade carrying a gun if no attack was planned), and along the way she met people who screamed "razzia" (raid). She cycled into the forest and hid her gun. When asked about her "Ausweis" (ID) at a checkpoint, Freddie, who by then was 19 years old, replied, "Habe Ich nicht, Ich bin noch kein 15 Jahre." ("I don't have one. I haven't turned 15 yet"). Because she looked much younger than she actually was, the Germans believed her and did not arrest her. She then probably went to Mari Andriessen's house to ask Truus if she knew where Hannie was.[122]

When it became clear that Hannie had not come home, the alarm was immediately sounded, both in the RVV and in other resistance groups. They were told that a girl fitting the description of Hannie Schaft had been brought into the Ortskommandantur office the night before and that she would have been brought to Amsterdam afterward. The RVV traveled all of the possible routes to Amsterdam. They were too late.

On April 17, 1945, Hannie was taken out of her cell by the German Mattheus Schmitz and the Dutch investigator, Maarten Kuijper (known for his arrests, his cooperation in the Silbertanne murders and his cruelty in interrogations). Hannie must have known this meant the end, because she screamed very hard and very long as she was escorted out of her cell. The imprisoned female doctor, Ada van Rossem, heard her screaming when she was taken away.[123]

Together with the Germans Korbs and Klüting, she was taken to Haarlem in a car, where at the Ortskommandantur a German soldier got into the car with a shovel. They drove to Overveen, via the Zeeweg, through the dunes and turned right just before Bloemendaal aan Zee toward the Spartelmeertje. Kuijper, and Schmitz took Hannie onto the dunes on foot.

It is unclear who shot Hannie. Ton Kors' book reports that Schmitz pointed his gun at Hannie's head, shot and missed. The bullet dealt a blow along her ear and Hannie shouted "Ouch!" According to a statement by SD top executive Willy Lages and SP top executive Emil Rühl, Hannie then turned around and shouted to Schmitz, "Idiot, I shoot better!" According to Truus Oversteegen's book, however, it was Lages who shot her. In any case, Kuijper then used his machine gun to end Hannie's life with a shot in the neck. A hole was dug in which they buried Hannie's body.[124]

Unaware of what was happening, Truus went to the Amsterdam House of Detention at the Weteringschans dressed in a German nurse's uniform. She told a story that she had been at the eastern front, that Hannie had been the sweetheart of a wounded naval officer and that the doctors thought he should see Hannie again. Unfortunately, the Weteringschans only held male prisoners, so Truus was referred to the Amstelveenseweg. Truus went there dressed as a Haarlem nurse of the Diaconessehuis. She pretended to be a very Christian woman and said that she thought she had to pay one last visit to Hannie. Truus was shown a book with the name J. J. Schaft crossed out, meaning, "Ist nicht mehr da" ("not there anymore"). The "Aufseherin" (female guard) who had shown the book to Truus walked away immediately. Truus fainted, and two large revolvers fell out of her pockets. Fortunately, they were not seen by anyone.[125]

Despite the agreement made between the Internal Armed Forces and the German occupiers not to carry out any more liquidations or executions, and despite the principle of not executing women, Hannie Schaft was put to death. The occupying forces must have realized the end of the war was approaching. Emil Rühl gave his motivation for executing Hannie in his statement to Ton Kors in Duisburg in 1975: "For us Hannie was a Mörderin, a terrorist who shot our people. Someone who hunted us and we hunted her. Kein Gerechtigkeit aber Vergeltung (Not justice but retribution)." The order for Hannie's execution had come from Willy Lages, but it is not clear whether he himself had ordered the execution or whether he had received a telephone order from "Obersturmbannführer" (senior assault or storm unit leader) Hans Kolitz from The Hague.[126]

Truus thought that Hannie had been taken away for interrogation. She did not know that Hannie had been executed. After the liberation, Truus returned with Philine Polak to the Amstelveenseweg to welcome Hannie as a liberated prisoner with a bunch of flowers, but Hannie did not show up.[127]

Harm Elsinga also went looking for Hannie. He was finally told by a Canadian officer, Captain Robertson, that Lages had been captured and that he was the only one who could help him further. Lages was questioned, and he told Harm that Hannie had been "erschossen" ("shot").[128]

Liberation Day, May 5, 1945, was not a day of celebration for the Elsinga family. Not only was Hannie missing and executed, as they learned later, but also their son Paul experienced something that he would have to carry with him the rest of his life. Liberation Day had started as a celebration. Paul was playing with a number of children from the Buitenrustlaan in the vicinity of the Houtplein and Dreef, the place where shelters were built during the war. These shelters were situated partly below and partly above the ground.

Mr. Kaufmann, a Swiss florist with a flower shop at Wagenweg 2 who had used his neutral Swiss identity to help people during the war, was arranging his flowers on the shelters, while the children, with Paul in their midst, danced, cheered and sang. All of a sudden, shots were heard. "How could that be?" Paul thought. "The war was over, wasn't it?" The shots continued. Germans were shooting randomly at the crowd from the opposite Wagenweg. Panic broke out. An older neighbor of Paul urged him to hide behind a tree. Paul ran to the tree but fell. At first Paul thought he had stumbled, but nothing could have been further from the truth. He was lying on the ground with his left leg in a strange curve. He had been shot, he realized; a bullet had gone through his left leg. The bone had been hit and shattered part of his leg. He did not see the German who shot him. There were more wounded people in the crowd, but miraculously, no one had been killed.[129]

Bystanders brought Paul into the Catholic Sancta Maria high school, at the Wagenweg. A nun did not want to help, she said that the school was not a hospital. Paul was put in the hallway and eventually was taken to the Diaconesse hospital at the Hazepaterslaan, where he was hospitalized for 12 weeks. Although his leg healed reasonably well, it caused him suffering throughout the rest of his life. Liberation Day became a very bitter pill for him.[130]

It was not until May 8, three days after Liberation Day, that the first Canadians entered Haarlem and the Germans were disarmed. The Canadians mainly settled in the southern part of the Haarlemmerhout.

Coincidentally, years later when Paul lived in Zwaag, he had a drink with his then neighbor, who told him that he too had been shot in his leg. This neighbor, Theo (last name unknown), had been hit in his leg by a stray bullet during the attack on Fake Krist that had bounced off the street and lodged in his leg. The bullet had been meant for Krist. Paul had heard these very shots from his school.[131]

Despite the celebrations of Liberation, Hannie's whereabouts were still unknown. Her parents initially thought she was still alive and that she was behind the IJssel line. On May 21, 1945, Hannie's mother went to see Mr. Sikkel, district attorney in Haarlem and Regional Commander of the Internal Armed Forces to inquire about her daughter. He told her that Hannie had been executed.

On May 22, 1945, Hannie's mother wrote a moving letter to Philine in which she announced the sad news:

"Dear Philine,

Yesterday morning we received the terrible message that our dear Joop was executed by the Gestapo on April 17. My darling has passed away and died for her ideals. Never to see her again, never to hear her, it is all so awful, so overwhelming, I can't describe it to you. See you soon.

Many regards and a kiss from aunt Jo and uncle P
Please inform her and your acquaintances."[132]

On the same day, Pieter Schaft wrote to his family:

"Dear all,

What we feared has become reality: our darling, our dear Joop, was killed by the Gestapo executioners at the very last moment (April 17, probably). We were struck with horror and I can't write anymore."[133]

Haarlem House of Detention the "Koepel," 2018. (Photo by Sophie Poldermans)

Cell 18 of Hannie Schaft at the "Koepel," 2018. (Photo by Sophie Poldermans)

West wing where women were held at Amsterdam House of Detention
at Amstelveenseweg, 2018. (Photo by Sophie Poldermans)

Hannie Schaft at Amsterdam House of Detention at Amstelveenseweg, just
before her execution, April 1945. (Courtesy of North Holland Archives)

Humanitarian food drops undertaken by Allied bomber crews,
April-May 1945. (Photo by Hans Poldermans)

Removal of German signs in the Haarlemmerhout,
May 1945. (Photo by Hans Poldermans)

Celebrating Liberation Day, walking around with German signs. Notice the
Dutch flags in front of the houses, May 1945. (Photo by Hans Poldermans)

Shaving heads of "Moffen girls" ("Kraut girls"), 1945. (Photo by Hans Poldermans)

Gathering crowd at Verwulft Haarlem looking at the shaving of the heads of "Moffen girls" ("Kraut girls"), May 1945. (Photo by Hans Poldermans)

*"Mauer-muur" in Haarlem welcoming Canadian troops,
May 1945. (Courtesy of North Holland Archives)*

Canadian troops, May 1945. (Courtesy of North Holland Archives)

PART III

TIME TO CONTEMPLATE

Chapter 8

After the War: How to Go On?

AFTER THE WAR, IN THE DUNES BEHIND OVERVEEN, THE bodies of hundreds of resistance fighters, including Hannie Schaft's body, were dug up.

On November 27, 1945, Jannetje Johanna (Hannie) Schaft was reburied at the honorary cemetery Eerebegraafplaats in Bloemendaal, in the same dunes where she had been shot. The reburial took place in the presence of Queen Wilhelmina (Queen from 1898-1948), Princess Juliana (Queen from 1948-1980) and Prince Bernhard. A memorial service was held in the Great Church in Haarlem.[134]

From there, the coffin with Hannie's body was taken to the Eerebegraafplaats, with enormous interest from onlookers. During this funeral procession, Truus walked behind the coffin. Paul Elsinga was a member of the Boy Scouts at the time and walked along in the procession about 100 meters behind the coffin, which was quite an achievement, since his left leg was still in a bandage. He completed the trip all the way to the Eerebegraafplaats.[135] Alongside the procession, Boy Scouts and members of the youth movement walked parallel and were positioned with an intermediate space of about 10 meters between them.

Wim Endert (b. January 18, 1933) was a 12-year-old boy at the time of Hannie Schaft's reburial. He lived at Hoofmanstraat 11 and stood along the Zijlweg with a group of schoolchildren when the procession passed by. Wim is one of the last living eyewitnesses of the reburial. He remembers the drums covered in black cloths and Chopin's Funeral March, which was played very well. The sad atmosphere, as well as the knowledge that Hannie Schaft had been shot and the funeral procession, made a huge impression on him. The children did not have to go back to school that day. They were allowed to play outside to process what they had seen. In the 1960s, Wim and his wife moved to Canada, but to this day this experience is still engraved in his memory.[136]

At the Eerebegraafplaats, Hannie Schaft is now the only woman among 371 men who are buried there. Posthumously, she received the Dutch Cross of Resistance. On this occasion, Queen Wilhelmina called Hannie Schaft the symbol of the national resistance against fascism. The Allied commander-in-chief, American General Eisenhower, also posthumously honored her with the special Medal of Freedom award.[137]

Sonja Frenk did not survive the war. In October 1943, she tried to flee to Switzerland but was betrayed on her escape route to Spain and was taken to concentration and extermination camp Auschwitz, where she died on November 24, 1943.[138]

Philine Polak did survive the war. She moved to the United States, where she married Erwin Lachman. After she completed her studies in international law, she worked for the United Nations Food and Agriculture Organization and the International Monetary Fund. She was also committed to women's rights.[139] On November 27, 2005, she was the keynote speaker at the National Hannie Schaft Commemoration. She passed away on March 17, 2018.

Frans van der Wiel was disillusioned after the war. Partly for this reason and also because of his fragile physical and mental health, he moved to Australia because of its warmer climate. At the request of Ton Kors, he drew up a written report in 1975 on the activities of the RVV and the role of Hannie Schaft in these activities. The report was recorded by his wife and written 30 years after the events took place. Because he was in very poor health, both physically and mentally, and was tormented by his experiences during the war, the report contains many generalities. Nevertheless, the report contains interesting details that I have included in this book. In Haarlem, the district of the resistance heroes also has a street named after Frans van der Wiel.

Both of the Oversteegen sisters survived the war. Truus married a fellow resistance fighter, Piet Menger. They had four children: Hannie (named after Hannie Schaft), Martin, Katinka and Peter. Truus became an artist and found this was a good way to deal with her memories and emotions about her activities in the resistance during the war. She also shared her experiences during the war in schools and in lectures.

Freddie married Jan Marius Dekker, an engineer at the Hoogovens in IJmuiden. They had three children: Tom, Jitte and Remy. She lived a more secluded life with her family.

Truus and Freddie always kept quiet about the number of liquidations and attacks they committed. When asked this question, Freddie said, "You shouldn't ask a soldier that question."[140]

How do you remain human under such inhuman conditions? Both Truus and Freddie emphasized they asked their liquidation targets if they were really who Truus and Freddie thought they were before liquidating them.

Also, Truus and Freddie always made sure that their liquidation targets did not know they would be attacked. In addition, they refused to carry out attacks involving children, and they also refused to carry out kidnappings of children.

Although a romantic image is sometimes portrayed of resistance fighters shooting their enemy, this is by no means the case in reality. Both Truus and Freddie were scarred for life. Truus said this of her experience: "I wasn't born to liquidate," and later, "Do you know what it does to your soul?"[141] Killing someone, "bruising" the family, as Freddie called it (families were disrupted), reprisals - all were very traumatizing. Both women were severely depressed at different stages of their lives. During several periods in her life, Freddie did not get out of bed for days; her husband had to take care of the children and do the housework. Truus even spent some time in a mental institution. Around May 4 and 5, when the Dutch official Commemoration Day and Liberation Day are celebrated, they both had intense nightmares and vivid memories of what had happened. They were haunted by the demons of their past. Both Truus and Freddie suffered from what nowadays would probably be diagnosed as post-traumatic stress disorder (PTSD). Hannie also most likely suffered from depression and PTSD after the death of Jan Bonekamp and in the weeks before her arrest.

Truus was much more open than Freddie about what had happened—with her family and friends and also with her art. Freddie's son, Remy Dekker, said that for his mother the war never stopped and was only over when she died.

Paul Elsinga survived the war as well, but his left leg kept troubling him because of his injury on Liberation Day. If someone survives a war as a child, it determines the rest of that child's life. Paul tells us that he labeled his life as "before the war" and "after the war." After the war, little was said about what had happened. Paul's five-years older brother, Ruud, never spoke about the war, and eventually the family lost contact with this older brother.

Not only did Paul suffer physically from the war due to his leg injury, he also developed anxiety from loud noises. The bombers that initially only came at night, but later during the day as well, left their mark on him. An incident at the bridge over the Spaarne river near his parents' home also fueled this fear considerably. Near this bridge, the Dieserink factory had been bombed and the enormous sound of explosions affected him greatly. He always remained scared of loud sounds.[142] Because of the war, Paul was also left with a strong aversion to anything that had to do with uniforms.

When asked if he slept badly, Paul initially answered that he slept fine. Then, in a quiet moment, he said, "Well, years ago my wife pointed out to me that I was fighting, as it were, in my sleep, that I slept restlessly." According to the family doctor, it was typical for children who experienced the war to suffer later, between 40 and 45 years of age.[143]

Paul reported to the Foundation for Civil War Victims (SBO) and went through a long procedure in order to become recognized as a civil war victim. He succeeded and receives a small monthly payment from the government. Paul is bitter about the fact that the law that made this possible was only adopted in 1984—much too late for some people. In his opening address to the National Hannie Schaft Commemoration of 2012, Paul explicitly drew attention to the survivors of the Second World War, in addition to those who had died.[144]

Procession at the reburial of Hannie Schaft, November 27,
1945. (Courtesy of North Holland Archives)

*Reburial of Hannie Schaft at Eerebegraafplaats Bloemendaal
in the presence of Queen Wilhelmina (Queen from 1898-1948),
November 27, 1945. (Courtesy of North Holland Archives)*

Eerebegraafplaats Bloemendaal, 2018. (Photos by Sophie Poldermans)

Gravestone of Jo (Hannie) Schaft, 2018. (Photo by Sophie Poldermans)

Chapter 9

———————

Political Aftermath

THE RESISTANCE AROSE FROM BOTH CHRISTIAN GROUPS and the Communist Party. Initially, no great importance was attached to the convictions behind the resistance work, but as time went by, it was indeed considered important.

After the war, the period prior to liberation was increasingly questioned. When it became clear that the Nazis were losing, more and more NSB people converted and/or joined the resistance. People who had worked closely with the Germans and people who held high positions were looking for opportunities to be labeled as patriotic. Resistance organizations were organized centrally, and more influence came from London.[145]

There were even rumors that, under the influence of the battle between Churchill and Stalin, the Dutch government in London felt threatened by everything that was politically left. Possibly, Queen Wilhelmina and Prince Bernhard had given the order from London to crack down on the political left. From this point of view, it is unclear who ordered the execution of Hannie Schaft. The Germans have always denied that they had anything to do with it, and, according to them, the Dutch were involved. It is suspected— and Truus was reasonably convinced of this—that the communist hunt from London had something to do with it, not so much the specific order to execute Hannie, but to defuse the political left in general. However, there is no hard evidence for this. Moreover, in connection with the "Velsen Affair," this is rather sensitive and involves major interests.[146]

After liberation, Freddie spent three months at the Loo Palace near Apeldoorn around Christmas 1945–1946. Queen Wilhelmina had set up two wings of her palace as a health resort for veterans and resistance fighters. Although Freddie did not want to go there at first, it turned out to be a good experience and she found real peace there. Freddie said of that experience: "I was treated like a princess."[147]

Freddie then worked for the Political Investigation Service (POD) for some time. This service was responsible for arresting people who had collaborated with the Germans during the war. Freddie traveled all over the country to pick up people who had been on the losing side in the war. She said of her work with the POD: "I caught so many NSB people. Through lists that were there, they were very easy to track down."[148]

Freddie soon noticed that people who had worked with the Germans were allowed to continue to hold senior positions. She told the authorities but was strongly advised to let that information go. This was unacceptable to her and she immediately resigned from the POD. Freddie felt terribly betrayed and remained very angry about this throughout her life. This is closely related to the "Velsen Affair."[149]

During the time of the Cold War (the unarmed struggle between the capitalist and the communist world that lasted from the Second World War until 1990), Hannie Schaft became the subject of a political fight. The youth organization of the Communist Party of the Netherlands (CPN), the General Dutch Youth Alliance (ANJV), had organized an annual commemoration in November (the time of the reburial of Hannie Schaft) at the Eerebegraafplaats in Bloemendaal, since the end of the war.[150]

On November 25, 1951, this commemoration, organized by the Hannie Schaft Committee, was to take place again. The board of the Eerebegraafplaats disagreed with the political content of the commemoration days that had been held in previous years and decided to set certain conditions—for example, that a commemoration should not have a demonstrative character and that it should serve the nation. That year, the board forbade having a commemoration day. At the same time, Mayor Cremers of Haarlem and Mayor Den Tex of Bloemendaal denied permission for a procession from the Dreef in Haarlem via the Zeeweg to the Eerebegraafplaats in Bloemendaal. Queen Wilhelmina's Commissioner De Vos van Steenwijk asked the Eerebegraafplaats to keep the fences closed because of the demonstrative nature of the event.[151]

For this reason, thousands of people organized their own commemoration that day by placing flowers in places in Haarlem that had to do with Hannie Schaft's life, for example at her parents' home and at the Jan Gijzenbrug at the Rijksstraatweg, where she had been arrested.

Despite the ban, about 4,000 people gathered at the foot of the Zeeweg in Overveen on November 25. Armored police vehicles tried to stop the crowd from going through with the event. A few people managed to get to Hannie's grave and left flowers there. Later, they were arrested.

Truus had this to say about that day: "When we, strengthened by the 'walk on comrades, they know that we are unarmed!' slowly approached the first armored car, it went like a moloch in our direction. The barrel of the gun in the turret turned toward us. An unbridled rage suddenly took hold of me. I let go of the wreath and walked toward the armored car. Tears flowed over my face. 'Are you really shooting at us, boy?' I shouted. 'I fought five years for your liberation; would you really shoot at me, at us?'"[152]

Truus and Freddie Oversteegen came from a communist environment (their mother had been a communist and was very socially active). Truus explained that she was a communist at first, but later she was one no longer. Freddie was less open about it.

Immediately after the war, both Truus and Freddie became targets of the political scene. Even after the war, they had to go into hiding because of their communist ideals. Truus bitterly said about this period: "What was an act of resistance before the war was a crime after the war. Our resistance work was not appreciated. On the contrary, we were condemned." It even went so far that both women were actually shot. Even though they weren't harmed physically, this was a terribly traumatizing experience for both of them. They had always fought for their ideal of a livable world and now that the war was over, they themselves became the target of a terrible political fight. Later in life, Truus' children also had to go into hiding because of serious threats. Policemen surveilled their family home and their phone was tapped in order to find the perpetrators.[153]

Starting in 1947, when people who had worked in the resistance could claim a resistance pension, Truus and Freddie were refused the pension because of their communist convictions. It was only in the 1960s that their pension was finally awarded to them.[154]

We do not know whether Hannie Schaft was a communist. There are still differences of opinion about Hannie's political background. She came from a socialist family, read Marxist literature and was internationally oriented. After the war, she had wanted to work for the League of Nations (the forerunner of the United Nations) in Geneva. She pursued ideals such as justice and equality. She was a member of the RVV, a resistance group that was largely communist, but it seems she was attracted to the group because she wanted to resist and not because of the communist ideas that some of the members of this group put forward.

Indeed, the idea that Hannie was a communist has never been proven. The RVV consisted of people from many different political backgrounds who had one thing in common: they wanted to resist the German occupiers. In that context, a person's political convictions make no difference.

After the Second World War and during the Cold War, there was little recognition for the people who had worked in the resistance and who had even the slightest link with communism. As mentioned earlier, this applied first and foremost to Truus and Freddie, but it also applied to people who were much further away from them. For example, after 46 years of loyal service in education, Harm Elsinga was refused a royal distinction for his work because he had had contact with communists - the people from the RVV who visited him. The fact that this was purely because of the work in the resistance and that there were no politics involved at all made no difference.[155] This led to bitterness for many members of the resistance and their offspring.

Partly because of these political tensions, various acts of resistance and resistance fighters were only recognized and praised much later. In addition, awards were not presented and monuments were not built until much later, when the most violent political storm began to fade away.

Immediately after the war, life was mainly devoted to reconstruction and progress, only later did it become possible to process and reflect on it. This also played a role in the relatively long delay before attention was paid to the resistance during the war.

As I witness the great interest in Hannie, Truus and Freddie and their resistance work in the media today, I see that their political convictions hardly play a role anymore, at least not in the recognition of their resistance work.

Freddie Oversteegen's identification card of the Political Investigation Service
(POD). She used her mother's last name, Van der Molen, on the identification
card, 2018. (Photo by Sophie Poldermans, private collection of Dekker family)

Chapter 10

The Annual National Hannie Schaft Commemoration

THERE IS A BRONZE STATUE OF HANNIE SCHAFT IN THE Kenaupark in Haarlem called "Woman in Resistance" which was unveiled on May 3, 1982 by Princess Juliana (Queen from 1948-1980). There was some discussion about whether there would be a statue of Hannie Schaft at all and, if so, who would make it. For years people discussed having a statue, but it was held back for political reasons. Eventually, the statue was made by none other than Truus Menger-Oversteegen. She had submitted five designs under a pseudonym and finally received the commission, and rightly so, because if anyone was eligible, she was. Truus was a sculptor, a resistance fighter and a Haarlem resident, and she had worked with Hannie Schaft in the resistance.[156]

When fewer and fewer people attended the annual commemoration of Hannie Schaft, a group of resistance fighters, including Truus Menger-Oversteegen and Freddie Dekker-Oversteegen and a number of organizations that emerged from the resistance, met to see how the commemoration could be revived. As a result of this initiative, the National Hannie Schaft

Commemoration Foundation was founded on June 3, 1996. In 2018, the foundation was renamed the National Hannie Schaft Foundation. The foundation organizes the annual National Hannie Schaft Commemoration on the last Sunday of November. This day was chosen because the reburial of Hannie Schaft had taken place on November 27, 1945.

The commemoration program is fixed. In the morning a wreath-laying ceremony takes place at Hannie Schaft's grave at the Eerebegraafplaats in Bloemendaal. In the afternoon a memorial service is organized in the Groenmarkt Church (former Padua Church) in Haarlem. Each year at the church a prominent Dutch person provides a lecture about Hannie Schaft, making her ideas and convictions relevant for the present time. Often personal stories and experiences are shared. Many prominent Dutch people have spoken at the annual commemoration including Hedy d'Ancona, Ed van Thijn, Job Cohen, Khadija Arib and Jacques Wallage. The commemoration is always accompanied by appropriate music.

At the end of the event, a silent march takes place from the church to the Kenaupark. A minute of silence is observed, after which the half-mast Dutch flag is hoisted and flown. Another wreath-laying ceremony takes place, this time at the statue, "Woman in Resistance." The mayors of Haarlem and Bloemendaal attend, as well as representatives of Haarlem's German sister city Osnabrück, the National Hannie Schaft Foundation, the Violette Szabo Foundation from the United Kingdom and various social organizations such as the National Committee 4 and 5 May, the Women's Concentration Camp Committee Ravensbrück and others.

This commemoration is a ceremony held to remember Hannie Schaft as a person, but also as a symbol for the (women's) resistance. The Hannie Schaft Foundation also seeks to raise awareness of the dangers of exclusion and discrimination by providing information in schools, organizing exhibitions and cooperating with institutions that have similar objectives.

Statue of Hannie Schaft "Woman in Resistance" by Truus Menger-Oversteegen (left), unveiled on May 3, 1982 by Princess Juliana (right; Queen from 1948-1980). (Courtesy of North Holland Archives)

Philine Lachman-Polak as keynote speaker at the National Hannie Schaft Commemoration, 2005. (Photo by Maarten Poldermans)

Sophie Poldermans as keynote speaker at the National Hannie Schaft Commemoration, 1998. (De Haarlemmer, December 3, 1998. Photo from photo agency Van den Ende/Boelo/Meijer)

Wreath-laying by Freddie Dekker-Oversteegen, Truus Menger-Oversteegen, Sophie Poldermans, and Mayor Jaap Pop at the National Hannie Schaft Commemoration, 2003. (Newspaper and photographer unknown)

Wreath-laying by Freddie Dekker-Oversteegen, Sophie Poldermans, and Truus Menger-Oversteegen at the National Hannie Schaft Commemoration, 2003. (Haarlems Weekblad, December 3, 2003. Photo by Willem Brand)

Silent march to the Kenaupark at the National Hannie Schaft Commemoration, 2003. Hedy d'Ancona, Mayor Jaap Pop, Maarten Poldermans, and Sophie Poldermans. (Haarlems Dagblad, December 1, 2003. Photo from United Photos De Boer/Poppe de Boer)

National Hannie Schaft Commemoration, showing wreath-laying at the statue of Hannie Schaft, "Woman in Resistance," 2018. (Photo by Sophie Poldermans)

Chapter 11

Fame and Distinction for Truus and Freddie Oversteegen

TRUUS WAS ALWAYS A VERY EXTROVERTED, ENGAGING and fun person. Her levelheadedness, self-mockery and positive attitude toward life made her very popular. She was direct, spoke the unvarnished truth and told lots of jokes. She loved to bring her ideals forward, and always kept resisting wars and fighting for their victims.

As mentioned earlier, Truus was very open about her experiences and she often spoke in schools to children and teenagers about the war. She was also a dedicated artist, and made both paintings and bronze sculptures. She created various war memorials, including the sculptures "Woman in Resistance" in Haarlem, "Leiden Women in Resistance" in Leiden, "Stone of Millions of Tears" in Rotterdam and "Frozen Tears" at the Memorial Centre Concentration Camp Westerbork.

Truus also created international war memorials, including a statue for the women from Srebrenica in Potocari, Bosnia-Herzegovina, and a statue at a hospital in Tanzania. Nelson and Winnie Mandela were present at the unveiling ceremony in Tanzania. Additionally, Truus set up a children's home for children with disabilities in Soweto, South Africa. Due to her active social involvement both at home and abroad, she enjoyed great fame.

Her husband, Piet Menger, stayed home and took care of their children. "My father allowed us to put the teabags on the coffee table," Hannie Menger remembered. "My mother was always on the road"—for exhibitions, lectures, awards. When she wasn't travelling, Truus could be found in her studio, painting and sculpting.

In the early 1970s, the entire family, with the exception of Hannie Menger, who was married and lived in Israel, took a trip around the world for one year. It was an unforgettable journey for all of them, despite the politically bad climate due to the Yom Kippur War.[157]

In 1982, Truus wrote her memoir, *Not Then, Not Now, Not Ever*, and in 2010 she published a collection of poems, *In My Mind's Eye*.

She met various heads of state and received several important awards for her resistance work, including an honorary medal from American General Eisenhower and the Yad Vashem award from Israeli Prime Minister Ben-Gurion. On her seventy-fifth birthday, she was appointed Officer in the Order of Oranje-Nassau in the Moses and Aäron Church in Amsterdam.

On April 15, 2014, she received, together with her sister Freddie, the Mobilization War Cross from Prime Minister Mark Rutte. A few months later, on June 12, 2014, near the Hannie Schaftstraat in Haarlem, a street was named after each of the sisters: the Truus Oversteegenstraat and the Freddie Oversteegenstraat. This was very special because normally streets are named only after people who have died.

Truus died on June 18, 2016, at the age of 92.

Freddie was sweet and gentle, very different from her sister. She made a very youthful, girlish impression throughout her entire life. But she could also be very fierce and at times very discontented.

At the expressed request of her husband, Jan Dekker, Freddie led a more withdrawn existence. Her way of dealing with the war was to focus entirely on her family. That did not always work out very well. Sometimes she would stay in bed for days when it all became too much for her, said her son, Remy Dekker.[158]

Freddie remained fierce and resisted various wars. For instance, she collected sewing machines during the Vietnam War, to be shipped via the port of IJmuiden. At that time her husband Jan was urged to talk Freddie into giving up these activities; otherwise, he could forget about a possible higher position at the Hoogovens in the future. Jan responded that his wife was independent and free to do whatever she wanted. Needless to say, he did not receive a promotion at that time.[159]

After Jan Dekker's retirement, Freddie and Jan travelled around the world in a motor home from December to well into May each year. In this way, they could distance themselves from their normal life and also escape from all discussions and (media) attention on the war and liberation. This annual trip with her husband was a way Freddie could be protected against her demons from the past, the nightmares that resurrected the memories of war and all the horrors that accompanied it. In the motor home and on the road, Freddie was a completely different person—much happier, carefree, open-minded and youthful.[160]

Because she had distanced herself from her normal life and the war, Freddie always stood in the shadow of her sister Truus, to some extent. She remained the little sister. Because of this, she sometimes felt as if she was not seen, even though she had done the same resistance work as her sister. When Hannie Schaft was awarded posthumously, it was Freddie who received the award on her behalf. This award was presented in 1981 by Queen Beatrix (Queen from 1980-2013) in the New Church in Amsterdam. Freddie and Truus did not receive any award then, which was frustrating, but there was another aspect to it. Men and women were not equally appreciated and praised for their resistance work. Freddie said this about the award ceremony: "I will never forget it. After the presentation of the medal, Beatrix came back. She said, embarrassed: 'Excuse me, I gave you the wrong box. I gave you a big box, which is for the men. The women get the little box. Ha, a woman gets a smaller award.'"[161]

The same thing happened when resistance pensions were granted. Freddie spoke about that policy: "Do people know that resistance men receive a higher resistance benefit than resistance women? I get less than a man. Why? No idea."[162] Freddie later said, "Women don't count. They still don't, that hasn't changed."[163]

It was all the more important for Freddie, therefore, that years later, on April 15, 2014, she received the Mobilization War Cross from Prime Minister Mark Rutte, together with Truus. A few months later, on June 12, 2014, a street in Haarlem was named after each of the sisters. It was the recognition that Freddie especially, had been looking for for so long. Truus and Freddie proudly looked at their names. Freddie said this about the naming of the streets after them: "I have the rental properties and Truus, the owner-occupied properties. Well, there's always someone who'll do you one better."[164]

After the death of her husband in 2003, Freddie began to talk cautiously about the war, but neither frequently nor in public. When her sister Truus died on June 18, 2016, she was the only survivor left of the resistance trio. She began to come forward and talk about her resistance work.

On September 5, 2018, one day before her ninety-third birthday, Freddie died. Her death received a great deal of attention, particularly from the international press. After an obituary in the *Washington Post*, all of the major international newspapers and radio and television stations, especially in the United States, Canada and the United Kingdom, as well as in India and Brazil, put Freddie in the spotlight.[165] It is remarkable that the woman who, while still alive, had always been in search of recognition now, after her death, was receiving it on such a large scale.

Truus Menger-Oversteegen, at an exhibition of her art work at North Holland Archives, May 3, 2008. (Photo by Jaap Pop)

Freddie Dekker-Oversteegen, 2000. (Photo by Maarten Poldermans)

Freddie Dekker-Oversteegen and Truus Menger-Oversteegen,
May 31, 2000. (Photo by Maarten Poldermans)

The sisters each get a street named after, Haarlem, June 12, 2014.
Truus Menger-Oversteegen, Freddie Dekker-Oversteegen, Maarten Poldermans,
and Mayor Bernt Schneiders. (Courtesy of National Hannie Schaft Foundation)

Freddie Dekker-Oversteegen and Truus Menger-Oversteegen receive
the Mobilization War Cross from Prime Minister Mark Rutte,
April 15, 2014. (Courtesy of National Hannie Schaft Foundation)

Epilogue

WHY IS IT SO IMPORTANT TO REMEMBER THESE THREE young women almost 75 years after the end of the Second World War and to keep their story alive? Freedom is a great gift. Unfortunately, this is not self-evident, and we must continue to cherish it. With the disappearance of the first generation of survivors of the war, it is all the more important to keep their stories alive, to pass them on and to learn from them. Exclusion and discrimination still happen all around us and on a large scale. The word *discrimination* literally means "making a distinction." That in itself is not a problem. It becomes a problem, however, if that distinction affects the equality of human beings. This gives the word a negative meaning. People are not the same, but they *are* equal. Every human being discriminates at times, for any reason. That is why it is very important to be wary of this danger that lurks in every one of us.

Wars are still occurring. It seems as if people have learned nothing from the past, which is a hard lesson. That is why it is of vital importance—in Hannie's case even literally—to let people look in the mirror and make them aware of this danger. What would you have done if you had been in the shoes of Hannie, Truus or Freddie? Would you have dared to make the same decisions?

I cannot answer that myself. Fortunately, I have never found myself in such a situation, and I sincerely hope that this will never happen. But if it does happen, the great challenge will be to remain human at all times, even and perhaps especially in times of inhumanity.

Looking at my own life, I can say that now that I have returned to live in Haarlem, I see the city from a new perspective, and the places that were central in the lives of Hannie, Truus and Freddie have become even more important for me. Almost daily I go for a stroll with my 10-month-old daughter, Sabine, through the Haarlemmerhout. She looks at the trees and animals through the radiant sunlight and coos with pleasure. It is such a huge contrast to the big, dark, scary forest that Freddie described. Sabine is a human being at the very beginning of her life. When strolling in the Haarlemmerhout, she is so close to the horrors of the past, to the place where people were liquidated, and to the spot where the remains of a high-ranking German SS officer could still be lying beneath her. Life and death are so close.

As a girl, I had an enormous need for strong female role models. Hannie Schaft and Truus and Freddie Oversteegen are perfect examples of strong female heroines. Today's society also needs similar icons. In my view, these three young women can still fulfill that role and will always continue to do so. We must pass on the stories of these courageous young women to future generations so that they, too, can make the right decisions.

Truus once wrote the following letter to me:

"Sophie,
To us, you are the future, the bearer of the new ideal, no racism, a livable world!

Thanks and love,
Truus Menger"[166]

Freddie scribbled underneath:

"*Lots of love,*
Freddie"[167]

I take their faith in me very seriously. For this reason, I wrote down the story of these three young women and their remarkable resistance work. In addition, I will continue to share their story in my speeches.

On the first page of Not Then, Not Now, Not Ever by Truus Menger, note by Truus Menger-Oversteegen and Freddie Dekker-Oversteegen to Sophie Poldermans. Translation: "Sophie, You are the future to us, the bearer of the new ideal, no racism, a livable world! Thanks and love, Truus Menger." Freddie scribbled underneath: "Lots of love, Freddie," 1998. (Photo by Sophie Poldermans)

Grote Markt, Great Church, Haarlem, 2019. (Photo by Sophie Poldermans)

*Draw bridge across the Spaarne river, Haarlem,
2019. (Photo by Sophie Poldermans)*

Acknowledgments

MY INTEREST IN HANNIE SCHAFT AND HER ROLE IN THE Dutch resistance during the Second World War arose in high school. When I had to write a thesis on a self-chosen topic for my history class, the topic was obvious for me: Hannie Schaft. I have always been grateful to my history teacher, Lucie Flothuis of the Stedelijk Gymnasium Haarlem, for her appreciation of my thesis, but especially for her encouragement to continue my research. I have indeed done so. Hannie Schaft and her fellow resistance fighters, Truus and Freddie Oversteegen, have always inspired me. Their stories and ideals have become a common thread in my personal and professional life.

I would like to thank the National Hannie Schaft Commemoration Foundation, now the National Hannie Schaft Foundation. The many board members I have met in recent years have inspired me to continue to embrace the ideas of Hannie Schaft and have strengthened me even more in my principles. Besides the founders of the Foundation, I would particularly like to mention Paul Elsinga, the son of Harm and Lien Elsinga, in whose house Hannie and Truus went into hiding, and Coen Hamers Sr. and Jo Post, who were part of the resistance group IJmuiden-Oost and in whose house the Foundation met for years. I am grateful that I got to know them and was able to work with them. Paul Elsinga and Coen Hamers Jr.

have also been extremely frank in a number of consecutive conversations and interviews.

I am deeply honored and thankful that I knew both Truus and Freddie Oversteegen for so long. This is historically very unique. I am very grateful to them for the inspiring and powerful stories they shared with me in conversations and interviews. Above all, I am grateful to them for allowing me to build a warm relationship with them. Both in my work and in my private life, these women and what they stood for will always be important.

Hannie Menger, the daughter of Truus who was named after Hannie Schaft, also deserves special thanks. I have built a wonderful relationship with her. She was able to tell me much about the resistance work of her mother and her aunt. She also told me a lot about the impact of their resistance work on her own life. Her warmth and levelheadedness were always greatly appreciated during board meetings of the Foundation, which she chaired for years.

Jaap Pop, Mayor of Haarlem from 1995–2006, took the portrait photo of me that appears on the back cover of this book and the portrait photos on my website (www.sophieswomenofwar.com). I would like to thank him very much for the beautiful pictures in the appropriate entourage of the Haarlemmerhout where Hannie, Truus and Freddie operated. The fact that Jaap Pop, as a prominent Haarlem resident, took these photos and still attends the annual National Hannie Schaft Commemoration, makes it extra special.

Joke Slootheer of design agency "Tekst in Vorm" did a great job in depicting all the relevant places of this book in the maps in the appendices.

Annelies Gallagher of Gallagher Translations has done a great job in translating my original Dutch book into English. I would like to thank her for her accurate and detailed translation and her involvement with and dedication to the contents of the book and its process of creation.

Greta Weber, a friend for life whom I met during my year in the United States as a foreign exchange student, helped me a great deal with editing and proof reading the manuscript of this book. I am forever thankful for her assessment and commentary, but above all for our friendship.

Last, but not least, I am very grateful to my family. My grandfather, Hans Poldermans, was a professional photographer. He lived with his wife, Elisabeth Heis, and his family in Heemstede for a long time and took great pictures of people and places of importance in the region during the Second World War. Both my grandparents told me about their own experiences during the war, for which I am very grateful.

My grandparents on my mother's side of the family also told me about their experiences during the war, especially my grandmother, Elisabeth van Vliet, who was very open with me about it, including her courier work for the Amsterdam resistance. My grandfather, André Veen had a printing business and taught me some important things regarding book printing. They both were very actively involved in raising me and always encouraged me to write and develop myself. I will always be very grateful to them.

My parents, Maarten Poldermans and Lida Veen and my brother, Cas Poldermans, encouraged me as a child to develop myself, to be independent and to choose my own path. They have always supported my work and provided valuable feedback. The same goes for my partner, Brum de Baat Doelman, and my daughter, Sabine de Baat Doelman. Without them, this book would never have come into being.

Maps of Europe and the Netherlands

(Maps by Joke Slootheer of "Tekst in Vorm")

Europe

The Netherlands

1. Haarlem
2. Amsterdam
3. Rotterdam
4. Arnhem
5. Enschede
6. Leiden
7. The Hague
8. Delfzijl
9. Concentration camp Westerbork
10. Concentration camp Vught
11. Zaandam
12. Limmen
13. Afsluitdijk
14. IJsselmeer
15. Krommenie
16. Loo Palace

Appendix 2

Map of North Holland

(Map by Joke Slootheer of "Tekst in Vorm")

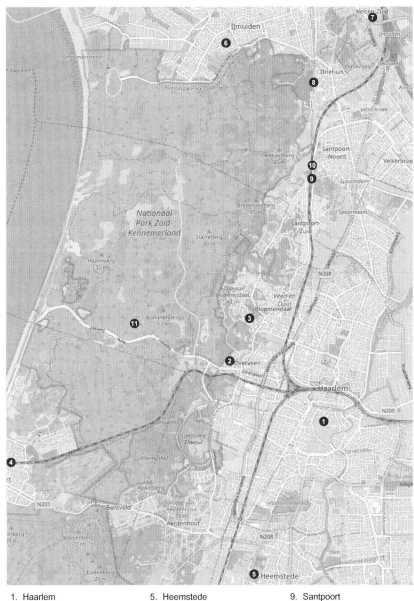

1. Haarlem	5. Heemstede	9. Santpoort
2. Overveen	6. IJmuiden	10. Netelbos
3. Bloemendaal	7. Velsen	11. Eerebegraafplaats
4. Zandvoort	8. Driehuis	

Appendix 3

Map of Haarlem and its Surrounding Areas

(Map by Joke Slootheer of "Tekst in Vorm")

1. Van Dortstraat 60, Haarlem: parental home of Jo (Hannie) from 1936.
2. Santpoorterplein, Haarlem: HBS-B of Jo (Hannie).
3. Stoops swimming pool, Overveen, where Jo (Hannie) stole identity cards.
4. Brouwersstraat 126, Haarlem: parental home of Truus and Freddie in 1940.
5. Olycanstraat 36, Haarlem: parental home of Truus and Freddie from 1940-1943.
6. Wagenweg 244-246, Haarlem: Mari Andriessen's house and RVV headquarters.
7. "House with the Statues," Haarlem: shooting lessons in backyard.
8. Haarlemmerhout, Haarlem: shooting lessons and liquidations.
9. Houtplein, Haarlem: "Loetje," bars and shelters.
10. Rembrandt cinema, Grote Markt, Haarlem.
11. Barteljorisstraat 19, Haarlem: Corrie ten Boom House.
12. Buitenrustlaan 22, Haarlem: Elsinga family, safe house of Hannie and Truus.
13. Spaarndamseweg, Haarlem: attack on Smit.
14. Schoterweg, Haarlem: attack on Willemse.
15. Westergracht, Haarlem: liquidation of Fake Krist.
16. Catholic Saint Bavo's Cathedral, Haarlem.
17. Rijkskweekschool, Leidschevaart 220, Haarlem.
18. Rijksleerschool, Schreveliusstraat 27, Haarlem: school of Harm and Paul Elsinga.
19. Railway bridge across the Spaarne river, Haarlem: failed attack.
20. Leidschevaart 18-22, Haarlem: Krelagehuis, liquidation of Willem Zirkzee.
21. Staten Bolwerk, Haarlem: attack on Ko Langendijk.
22. Former Café Spoorzicht, Haarlem, where Hannie and Truus hid after their attack on Ko Langendijk.
23. Schoterstraat, Haarlem: liquidation of Gerdo Bakker.
24. Twijnderslaan, Haarlem: attack on Madame Sieval.
25. Bosch en Hovenstraat, Haarlem: liquidation of Dicky Wafelbakker.
26. "Mauer-muur" at the Jan Gijzenbrug at the Rijksstraatweg, Haarlem, where the arrest of Hannie took place.
27. Ripperdakazerne, Kleverlaan, Haarlem.
28. Ortskommandantur, Fonteinlaan, Haarlem.
29. Haarlem House of Detention the "Koepel," Oostvest, Haarlem.
30. Wagenweg 2: flower shop of Mr. Kaufmann, Haarlem.
31. Great Church, Haarlem.
32. Eerebegraafplaats, Bloemendaal.
33. Kenaupark, Haarlem, sculpture "Woman in Resistance."
34. Hannie Schaftstraat, Haarlem.
35. Truus Oversteegenstraat, Haarlem.
36. Freddie Oversteegenstraat, Haarlem.
37. Frans van der Wielstraat, Haarlem.
38. Corner Tooropkade-Eerelmanstraat, Heemstede: attack on Piet Faber.
39. Groenmarkt Church, location of National Hannie Schaft Commemoration.

Chronology of the Second World War

Below is an overview of important events prior to and during the Second World War. *Events in the Netherlands are printed in italics.*

1921, Germany: Foundation of the SA ("Sturm Abteilung"). This was a military organization of the NSDAP (National Socialist German Workers Party) that had the task of protecting party meetings and fighting opponents such as communists and socialists.

1924, Germany: Establishment of the SS ("Schutz Staffel"). This was an elite unit of the NSDAP, created from the SA. The original task of this organization was to protect the leaders of the party, especially Adolf Hitler. Soon SS departments were created with a purely military task, the "Waffen SS."

1931, Germany: Founding of the SD ("Sicherheits Dienst") by Heinrich Himmler (1900–1945). This was a National Socialist intelligence and espionage service that was part of the SS. The SD worked closely with the SP ("Sicherheits Polizei"). The task of this organization was to track down all categories of opponents of the regime and to deport and destroy them.

1931, the Netherlands: Founding of the NSB (National Socialist Movement) by Anton Adriaan Mussert (1894–1946).

1933, Germany: On January 30, Adolf Hitler (Austrian-born German politician) was sworn in as Chancellor. Hitler was the leader of the NSDAP, which was the largest party in Germany in July and November 1932. Hitler was commissioned to form a new government.

1934, Germany: On June 30, Hitler had the radical leaders of the SA, including Ernst Röhm, killed. The SA then quickly lost significance.

1934, Germany: On August 2, Hitler became President of the Reich and chose the title "Führer."

September 30, 1938: The Munich Conference was held. Participants were Hitler (Germany), Mussolini (Italy), Chamberlain (United Kingdom) and Daladier (France). The Munich Agreement was signed. Chamberlain thought this would prevent war with Germany.

September 1, 1939: Germany invaded Poland.

September 3, 1939: The United Kingdom and France declared war on Germany.
Beginning of the Second World War

April, 1940: Germany occupied Denmark and Norway.

May 10, 1940, the Netherlands: German troops attacked the Netherlands. They conquered the Waalhaven airport, a part of Rotterdam-Zuid, using the bridge over the Maas and the Moerdijk bridge.

May 11, 1940, the Netherlands: North Brabant, despite France's help, was trampled. The attack on the Grebbe line (near Rhenen) and the Kornwerderzand fort (Afsluitdijk) started.

May 13, 1940, the Netherlands: Queen Wilhelmina and the Dutch government fled to London in the United Kingdom.

May 14, 1940, the Netherlands: Rotterdam was bombarded.

May 15, 1940, the Netherlands: The Dutch army, with the exception of the troops in Zeeland, capitulated.

May 18, 1940, the Netherlands: Haarlem born Bernard IJzerdraat called for resistance via the "Geuzenbericht" in Rotterdam.

May 19, 1940, the Netherlands: Zeeland was evacuated by the Dutch troops.

May 29, 1940, the Netherlands: The Austrian Arthur Seyss-Inquart was appointed as Commissioner of the Reich in the Netherlands.

June 29, 1940, the Netherlands: "Carnation Day." On the occasion of the birthday of Prince Bernhard, many Dutch people showed their anti-German attitude by wearing a carnation—the symbol of the prince.

September 15, 1940, the Netherlands: Founding of the Dutch SS by Anton Adriaan Mussert. The name of the Dutch SS was later changed to "Germanic SS in the Netherlands."

October, 1940, the Netherlands: All service officials were obliged to sign an "Aryan declaration"—proof of Germanic origin. This was one of the first signs of the systematic exclusion of Jews. Most of the officials did this.

During 1940, the Netherlands: The first resistance organizations were established: De Geuzen, de Waarheid ("Truth") and the Legioen van Oud-Frontstrijders. Illegal newspapers were published, help was offered to people in hiding and people became involved in espionage and armed resistance.

February 25, 1941, the Netherlands: "February Strike." This was the first large-scale resistance action against the German occupation and represented a turning point. This strike was the only massive and open protest against the persecution of Jews in occupied Europe. It stirred up resistance throughout the Netherlands.

June 22, 1941: Germany attacked the Soviet Union.

Autumn 1941, the Netherlands: Measures against Jews were strengthened, and Jews were banned from becoming members of the student association.

December 7, 1941: A surprise attack was made by the Japanese Imperial Navy, led by Admiral Isoroku Yamamoto, on the American naval base at Pearl Harbor in Hawaii. The attack was intended to destroy most of the United States fleet so that Japan would have free rein in the Pacific Ocean. The United States declared war on Japan.

December 8, 1941: The Netherlands declared war on Japan.

December 11, 1941: Hitler officially declared war on the United States.

May 9, 1942, the Netherlands: Jews were forced to wear a yellow star.

July 1942, the Netherlands: The deportation of Jews began. With the help of the Jewish Council, Dutch Jews were registered to be employed in Germany and Poland. Via the Dutch concentration camp Westerbork, however, they were taken to concentration and extermination camps such as Auschwitz, Majdanek, Ravensbrück, Neuengamme, Bergen-Belsen, Sobibor and Treblinka. Almost 100,000 people died in these concentration camps.

The LO (National Organization for Assistance to People in Hiding) was formed to provide addresses of places to hide, forged personal identification cards and ration cards by attacks on distribution offices.

February 6, 1943, the Netherlands: Every student was required to sign the so-called declaration of loyalty. Eighty-five per cent of the students refused and were subsequently employed in Germany or had to go into hiding.

March 27, 1943, the Netherlands: An attack was made on the Amsterdam population register to confuse the German administration. The perpetrators, among whom was Gerrit van der Veen, were betrayed, and shot.

April 29, 1943, the Netherlands: April-May strikes were made following the captivity of Dutch soldiers.

Autumn 1943, the Netherlands: The National Assault Team (LKP) came into being from various armed organizations.

June 6, 1944: "D-day." The Allied armies landed in Normandy and advanced to Germany from three sides: Normandy, southern France/Italy and Russia.

September 5, 1944, the Netherlands: "Mad Tuesday." Radio Oranje reported that the Allies were at Breda, in the southern part of the Netherlands. Germans and NSB officers fled en masse, and people in hiding showed them-selves openly on the streets.

September 17, 1944, the Netherlands: The Battle of Arnhem was lost. Operation Market Garden under the command of British general Montgomery failed. The Germans beat back an Allied offensive. Prime Minister Gerbrandy called, from the government in exile in London, for a general railway strike to support the operations. The Germans then claimed all means of transport, which seriously stagnated all transportation. This led to major food shortages in the west, which resulted in the beginning of the Dutch famine or Hunger Winter (1944–1945).

In Haarlem-Noord residents had to evacuate, so many people in hiding had to find new safe houses. Evacuation plans were also prepared for IJmuiden, Bloemendaal, Santpoort, Driehuis and Beverwijk so that the Germans could better defend their access to the North Sea Canal in case of a possible Allied invasion.

September 22, 1944, the Netherlands: In Haarlem, only two hours of gas a day was supplied to the residents of the city.

October 9, 1944, the Netherlands: The electricity supply in Haarlem was cut off. Partly because of this, the actions of the resistance were intensified.

October 1944, the Netherlands: The western part of North Brabant and Zeeland was liberated.

April 29, 1945, the Netherlands: The Allies dropped food above the west of the Netherlands.

May 2, 1945: Germany Berlin fell to the Soviets.

May 5, 1945, the Netherlands: In Wageningen, German general Blaskowitz signed, in front of Canadian general Foulkes and Prince Bernhard, the capitulation of all German troops present in the Netherlands. Liberation Day.
The Second World War ends in the Netherlands.

May 7, 1945: General Jodl surrendered unconditionally all German troops in General Eisenhower's headquarters in Reims. General Jodl's capitulation was repeated on May 9th at the Russian headquarters in Berlin-Karlshorst, in front of Marshal Zhukow.
The Second World War ends in Europe.

May 8, 1945: Canadian troops arrived in Haarlem.

August 6, 1945: The United States dropped an atomic bomb on the Japanese city of Hiroshima.

August 8, 1945: The Soviet Union declared war on Japan.

August 9, 1945: The United States dropped an atomic bomb on the Japanese city of Nagasaki.

August 15, 1945: Japan capitulated.

September 2, 1945: The Japanese Instrument of Surrender was signed by General MacArthur of the Allies and by Japan's foreign minister, Mamoru Shigemitsu, on behalf of the Japanese Emperor Hirohito, aboard the USS *Missouri*. The Empire of Japan formally surrendered.
The Second World War ends globally.

Chronology of the Lives and Resistance work of Hannie, Truus and Freddie

September 16, 1920	Jannetje Johanna (Jo) (Hannie) Schaft was born.
August 29, 1923	Truus Oversteegen was born.
1924	Jo (Hannie) made a drawing in kindergarten with the word *Peace* on the facade.
September 6, 1925	Freddie Nanda Oversteegen was born.
December 6, 1927	Jo's (Hannie's) sister Annie, who was five years older, died of diphtheria.
1932	Jo (Hannie) went to the HBS-B high school at the Santpoorterplein.
1934	The Oversteegen family hosted German refugees via the Committee de Rode Hulp.
1938	Jo (Hannie) started studying law at the University of Amsterdam.

1939	Jo (Hannie) sent parcels to imprisoned Polish officers via the International Red Cross after the German invasion of Poland.
1941	Truus and Freddie joined the Council of Resistance.
1942	Jo (Hannie) stole identity cards for Jewish people.
1943, spring	Jo (Hannie) joined the Council of Resistance.
1943	Hannie, Truus and Freddie met.
November 24, 1943	Hannie, Jan Bonekamp, Jan Brasser and Jan Bak attempted to disable the PEN power plant.
January 20, 1944	Hannie, Jan Heusdens, Cor Rusman and Co Kooyman attempted to blow up the Rembrandt cinema.
June 8, 1944	Hannie and Jan Bonekamp liquidated Piet Faber.
June 21, 1944	Hannie and Jan Bonekamp attacked Ragut; Jan Bonekamp was injured in the attack and subsequently died of his injuries.
September 5, 1944	Truus and Jan Heusdens attacked Fake Krist's subordinate, Smit; they failed in their attack on Fake Krist; Hannie and Cor Rusman attacked another subordinate of Fake Krist, Willemse.
October 25, 1944	"Black Kees" (Gommert Krijger) liquidated Fake Krist.
March 1, 1945	Hannie and Truus liquidated Willem Zirkzee.

March 15, 1945	Hannie and Truus attacked Ko Langendijk.
March 19, 1945	Hannie and Truus liquidated Gerdo Bakker.
March 21, 1945	Hannie and Truus attacked Madame Sieval; Hannie was arrested.
April 13, 1945	Truus and Freddie liquidated Dicky Wafelbakker.
April 17, 1945	Hannie was executed and buried.
November 27, 1945	Hannie was reburied.
November 25, 1951	The Hannie Schaft commemoration was prohibited.
May 3, 1982	The statue, "Woman in Resistance," was unveiled in the Kenaupark.
June 3, 1996	The National Hannie Schaft Commemoration Foundation was established (as of 2018, the National Hannie Schaft Foundation).
April 15, 2014	The Mobilization War Cross was awarded to Truus and Freddie.
June 18, 2016	Truus died.
September 5, 2018	Freddie died.

Abbreviations

Note that official Dutch names have been translated into English for the reader's benefit.

ANJV	General Dutch Youth Alliance
AVSV	Amsterdam Female Student Association
BS	Internal Armed Forces
CPN	Communist Party of the Netherlands
FN gun	Gun of the brand "Fabrique Nationale," Herstal, Belgium
GEMMA	"Gemmare e minoribus appetinus" ("From small things we strive for bigger things")
Gestapo	Secret State Police
HBS-B	High school—Beta (science subjects)

LKP	National Assault Team (resistance group founded by LO – see below)
LO	National Organization for Assistance to People in Hiding
NSB	National Socialist Movement
NSDAP	National Socialist German Workers Party
NZHTM	North-South-Holland Tramway Society
PEN	Provincial Electric Company of North Holland
POD	Political Investigation Service
PTSD	Post-Traumatic Stress Disorder
RVV	Council of Resistance
SA	"Sturm Abteilung" (Storm Department)
SBO	Foundation Civil War Victims
SD	"Sicherheits Dienst" (Security Service)
SDAP	Social Democratic Workers Party
SP	"Sicherheits Polizei" (Security Police)
SS	"Schutz Staffel" (Protection Squadron)

V1	"Vergeltungswaffe 1" or Vengeance Weapon 1, a kind of unmanned flying bomb
UN	United Nations

Notes

1   Hammann, *Hannie*, 18–19.

2   Kors, *Hannie Schaft*, 21.

3   Kors, *Hannie Schaft*, 16–17.

4   Kors, *Hannie Schaft*, 25.

5   Kors, *Hannie Schaft*, 30.

6   Kors, *Hannie Schaft*, 31 and 39.

7   Kors, *Hannie Schaft*, 33.

8   Kors, *Hannie Schaft*, 35.

9   Kors, *Hannie Schaft*, 35.

10   Kors, *Hannie Schaft*, 37–38.

11   Kors, *Hannie Schaft*, 43.

12   Kors, *Hannie Schaft*, 44.

13   Kors, *Hannie Schaft*, 44.

14   Kors, *Hannie Schaft*, 52; Hammann, *Hannie*, 37.

15   O'Leary, "'Her war never stopped': the Dutch teenager who resisted the Nazis," September 23, 2018.

16   Oversteegen, Truus, interview by Sophie Poldermans. (February 28, 1998).

17   Oversteegen, Truus, interview by Sophie Poldermans. (February 28, 1998).

18   Oversteegen, Truus, interview by Sophie Poldermans. (February 28, 1998).

19   Menger, *Toen Niet, Nu Niet, Nooit*, 34–37; *Andere Tijden. Gewapend verzet*. Directed by Yaèl Koren (NTR-VPRO, 2012).

20   Menger, *Toen Niet, Nu Niet, Nooit*, 38–41.

21   *Omdat het moet*. Directed by Mieke Benda (National Hannie Schaft Commemoration Foundation, 2014).

22   Jacobs, *Palet van verzet*, 135.

23   Oversteegen, Truus, interview by Sophie Poldermans. (February 28, 1998).

24   Menger, *Toen Niet, Nu Niet, Nooit*, 84–86.

25   Oversteegen, Truus, interview by Sophie Poldermans. (February 28, 1998).

26   *Hannie Schaft: het meisje met het rode haar*. Directed by Ineke Hilhorst (AVRO, 1980).

27   Oversteegen, Truus, interview by Sophie Poldermans. (February 28, 1998).

28   *Andere Tijden. Gewapend verzet*. Directed by Yaèl Koren (NTR-VPRO, 2012).

29   Van der Wiel, Frans. Melbourne, March 28, 1975.

30   *Hannie Schaft: het meisje met het rode haar*. Directed by Ineke Hilhorst (AVRO, 1980).

31   Van der Wiel, Frans. Melbourne, March 28, 1975.

32   Kors, *Hannie Schaft*, 58.

33   Oversteegen, Truus, interview by Sophie Poldermans. (February 28, 1998).

34   Jacobs, *Palet van verzet*, 135.

35   *Omdat het moet*. Directed by Mieke Benda (National Hannie Schaft Commemoration Foundation, 2014).

36   Van der Wiel, Frans. Melbourne, March 28, 1975.

37   *Andere Tijden. Gewapend verzet*. Directed by Yaèl Koren (NTR-VPRO, 2012).

38   *Omdat het moet*. Directed by Mieke Benda (National Hannie Schaft Commemoration Foundation, 2014).

39   Kors, *Hannie Schaft*, 130.

40   Van der Wiel, Frans. Melbourne, March 28, 1975.

41   Menger, Hannie, interview by Sophie Poldermans. (August 13, 2018).

42   *Twee zussen in verzet*. Directed by Manon Hoornstra and Thijs Zeeman (MAX, 2016); Oversteegen, Truus, interview by Sophie Poldermans. (February 28, 1998); Menger, *Toen Niet, Nu Niet, Nooit*, 111–115.

43   Oversteegen, Truus, interview by Sophie Poldermans. (February 28, 1998).

44   Oversteegen, Truus, interview by Sophie Poldermans. (February 28, 1998).

45   Oversteegen, Truus, interview by Sophie Poldermans. (February 28, 1998).

46   Oversteegen, Truus, interview by Sophie Poldermans. (February 28, 1998).

47   Oversteegen, Truus, interview by Sophie Poldermans. (February 28, 1998).

48   Kors, *Hannie Schaft*, 82.

49   National Hannie Schaft Commemoration Foundation, *Fietsen langs het verzet*, 15.

50   *Andere Tijden. Gewapend verzet.* Directed by Yaèl Koren (NTR-VPRO, 2012).

51   Kors, *Hannie Schaft*, 90; Ten Boom, Sherrill, and Sherrill, *The Hiding Place*, 1974; *The History of the Ten Boom Family*, Corrie ten Boom House, November 2018. http://www.corrietenboom.com (accessed November 3, 2018).

52   Kors, *Hannie Schaft*, 90; National Hannie Schaft Commemoration Foundation, *Fietsen langs het verzet*, 14–15; Van Woerden, Bob (Casper), n.d.

53   Kors, *Hannie Schaft*, 90; National Hannie Schaft Commemoration Foundation, *Fietsen langs het verzet*, 14–15; Van Woerden, Bob (Casper), n.d.

54   *The History of the Ten Boom Family,* Corrie ten Boom House, November 2018. http://www.corrietenboom.com (accessed November 3, 2018).

55   Van Woerden, Bob (Casper), n.d.

56   Kors, *Hannie Schaft*, 90.

57   Kors, *Hannie Schaft*, 90–91.

58   *Hannie Schaft: het meisje met het rode haar.* Directed by Ineke Hilhorst (AVRO, 1980).

59   Kors, *Hannie* Schaft, 98-99.

60   Original article in Dutch:

"Verwildering:"

Men moge de lafhartigheid van den moord op een weerloos mensch in het licht stellen en gruwen bij de gedachte, dat het hier een <u>vrouw</u> is, die zich vergrijpt aan het leven, het leven tot de voortbrenging waarvan God de vrouw roept.

61   Kors, *Hannie Schaft*, 103.

62   Menger, *Toen Niet, Nu Niet, Nooit*, 99.

63   Kors, *Hannie Schaft*, 103.

64   Kors, *Hannie Schaft*, 104–106.

65   Van der Wiel, Frans. Melbourne, March 28, 1975.

66   Menger, *Toen Niet, Nu Niet, Nooit*, 99–101.

67   Menger, *Toen Niet, Nu Niet, Nooit*, 101.

68   Van der Wiel, Frans. Melbourne, March 28, 1975.

69   Kors, *Hannie Schaft*, 107.

70   Kors, *Hannie Schaft*, 91.

71   Menger, *Toen Niet, Nu Niet, Nooit*, 185; Kors, *Hannie Schaft*, 110.

72   Elsinga, Paul, interview by Sophie Poldermans. (November 6, 2018).

73   Elsinga, Paul, interview by Sophie Poldermans. (November 6, 2018).

74   Elsinga, Paul, interview by Sophie Poldermans. (November 6, 2018).

75   Hammann, *Hannie*, 52.

76   Kors, *Hannie Schaft*, 118–120. Original Dutch letter:

"*Lieve Philine,*

Aangezien mijn pen nog steeds lekt, schrijf ik maar met potlood. Ik heb nl. net mijn handen gewassen. Dat je zo lang niets van me gehoord hebt, is niet mijn schuld: de vorige brief (van 2 weken geleden) moest op een gegeven moment verscheurd worden. Ik vind het erg fijn, dat je het zo goed maakt. Het had ook anders kunnen zijn, en héél anders! I am in the very best of health. Sinds een paar weken ben ik weer in functie, net op tijd, want anders was ik gek geworden. Mijn geestelijke toestand is nog steeds allerbedroevendst: ik kan geen boek lezen, noch roman, noch studieboek. In mijn vrije tijd brei ik een kous!! Komt de situatie je niet bekend voor?

Ik ben aanzienlijk minder hard dan ik gedacht had: de kennismaking met de dood is niet meegevallen. En in dit geval was ze wel bijzonder direct. De werkloosheid daarna heeft me ook niet bepaald gekalmeerd. En nu is het te laat. Ik zal nog pogingen doen om de brokstukken van mijn oude ik te redden. Maar dat gaat waarschijnlijk niet meer. De mensen zijn in zo'n feeststemming. Ik zit er bij als een glimlachende Boeddha en men verwacht van mij, dat ik óók in feeststemming ben. Het liefst zou ik vloeken. Helaas kan ik dat alleen bij jou en nog een paar mensen. Als straks de oorlog afgelopen is, en jij zit in een hoekje te huilen, kom ik bij jou deze bezigheid ook verrichten. Lieve kind, ik zou graag bij je komen, maar je begrijpt, dat ik op het ogenblik niet weg kan. Het zal dus wel "na de oorlog" worden. Wanneer zal dat zijn? Misschien op mijn verjaardag. Nu word ik melodramatisch: mocht ik je helemaal niet meer zien, dan geef ik je hier enige richtlijnen voor de toekomst a. Solidariteit b. Voortzetting van ons aller werk. Wij zijn nu eenmaal een twee-eenheid, en intellect is hard nodig voor de zaak, en onze maatschappelijke ombouw (of afbraak – opbouw) c. Denk niets lafs van mijn vriend. Hij heeft zich prachtig gedragen. Het was te wensen, dat er meer van zulke mensen waren en overbleven. Hij was één van de fijnste kerels, die ik ooit heb ontmoet. Onthou dit, het is heel belangrijk. Philine, tot spoedig ziens.

Hartelijke groeten,

Jo.

P.S. Ik vang bijna dagelijks vlooien!"

77   Menger, *Toen Niet, Nu Niet, Nooit*, 104.

78   Menger, *Toen Niet, Nu Niet, Nooit*, 177.

79   Hammann, *Hannie*, 53.

80   Kors, *Hannie Schaft*, 127–128.

81   Kors, *Hannie Schaft*, 128.

82   Kors, *Hannie Schaft*, 122.

83   Kors, *Hannie Schaft*, 124.

84   Kors, *Hannie Schaft*, 125.

85   Elsinga, Paul, interview by Sophie Poldermans. (November 6, 2018).

86   Kors, *Hannie Schaft*, 132; Menger 1982, 129–130.

87   Elsinga, Paul, interview by Sophie Poldermans. (November 6, 2018).

88   Kors, *Hannie Schaft*, 134; Menger, *Toen Niet, Nu Niet, Nooit*, 131–132.

89   National Hannie Schaft Commemoration Foundation, *Fietsen langs het verzet*, 10.

90   Elsinga, Paul, interview by Sophie Poldermans. (November 6, 2018).

91   Kors, *Hannie Schaft*, 141–152; Von Benda Beckmann, *De Velser Affaire*, 2013; *Andere Tijden. Gewapend verzet.* Directed by Yaèl Koren (NTR-VPRO, 2012).

92   *Hannie Schaft: het meisje met het rode haar.* Directed by Ineke Hilhorst (AVRO, 1980).

93   Kors, *Hannie Schaft*, 131.

94   Menger, *Toen Niet, Nu Niet, Nooit*, 143–147; Hammann, *Hannie,* 61.

95   Hamers, Coen Jr., interview by Sophie Poldermans. (December 12, 2018).

96   Hamers, Coen Jr., interview by Sophie Poldermans. (December 12, 2018); *OVERVAL OP Commando-Post (CP) op 16 februari 1945. Een onderbelicht verhaal uit het bezette IJmuiden-Oost,* Coen Hamers Jr., December 2018. http://www.hamers.nl/genealog/verhalen (accessed December 12, 2018).

97   Hamers, Coen Jr., interview by Sophie Poldermans. (December 12, 2018); *OVERVAL OP Commando-Post (CP) op 16 februari 1945. Een onderbelicht verhaal uit het bezette IJmuiden-Oost,* Coen Hamers Jr., December 2018. http://www.hamers.nl/genealog/verhalen (accessed December 12, 2018).

98   Hamers, Coen Jr., interview by Sophie Poldermans. (December 12, 2018); *OVERVAL OP Commando-Post (CP) op 16 februari 1945. Een onderbelicht verhaal uit het bezette IJmuiden-Oost*, Coen Hamers Jr., December 2018. http://www.hamers.nl/genealog/ verhalen (accessed December 12, 2018); Von Benda Beckmann, *De Velser Affaire*, 228–229.

99   Hammann, *Hannie*, 62.

100   Kors, *Hannie Schaft*, 169–171; Menger, *Toen Niet, Nu Niet, Nooit*, 133–142; *Hannie Schaft: het meisje met het rode haar*. Directed by Ineke Hilhorst (AVRO, 1980).

101   *Hannie Schaft: het meisje met het rode haar*. Directed by Ineke Hilhorst (AVRO, 1980).

102   *Hannie Schaft: het meisje met het rode haar*. Directed by Ineke Hilhorst (AVRO, 1980).

103   Kors, *Hannie Schaft*, 172.

104   Menger, *Toen Niet, Nu Niet, Nooit*, 162–167.

105   Kors, *Hannie Schaft*, 190; *Andere Tijden. Gewapend verzet*. Directed by Yaèl Koren (NTR-VPRO, 2012).

106   Ten Boom, Sherrill, and Sherrill, *The Hiding Place*, 1974.

107   Van Woerden, Bob (Casper), n.d.

108   Van Woerden, Bob (Casper), n.d.

109   National Hannie Schaft Commemoration Foundation, *Fietsen langs het verzet*, 8; *Andere Tijden. Gewapend verzet*. Directed by Yaèl Koren (NTR-VPRO, 2012).

110   Van Woerden, Bob (Casper), n.d.; Schipper, Kees, 2004.

111   Schipper, Kees, 2004.

112   Schipper, Kees, 2004.

113   Schipper, Kees, 2004.

114 *Andere Tijden. Gewapend verzet.* Directed by Yaèl Koren (NTR-VPRO, 2012).

115 Oversteegen, "Letter from Truus Oversteegen to Ms. Koorn," May 20, 1991.

116 Kors, *Hannie Schaft*, 168–176.

117 Kors, *Hannie Schaft*, 176–178.

118 Kors, *Hannie Schaft*, 176–178.

119 Menger, *Toen Niet, Nu Niet, Nooit*, 184.

120 Elsinga, Paul, interview by Sophie Poldermans. (November 13, 2018).

121 Kors, *Hannie Schaft*, 181; *Hannie Schaft: het meisje met het rode haar.* Directed by Ineke Hilhorst (AVRO, 1980).

122 *Omdat het moet.* Directed by Mieke Benda (National Hannie Schaft Commemoration Foundation, 2014).

123 Kors, *Hannie Schaft*, 201.

124 Kors, *Hannie Schaft*, 201–202.

125 Menger, *Toen Niet, Nu Niet, Nooit*, 187; 193–199.

126 Kors, *Hannie Schaft*, 190–191.

127 Menger, *Toen Niet, Nu Niet, Nooit*, 200–204.

128 Kors, *Hannie Schaft*, 205; Elsinga, Paul, interview by Sophie Poldermans. (November 6, 2018).

129 Elsinga, Paul, interview by Sophie Poldermans. (November 6, 2018).

130 Elsinga, Paul, interview by Sophie Poldermans. (November 6, 2018).

131 Elsinga, Paul, interview by Sophie Poldermans. (November 6, 2018).

132 Letter from Hannie Schaft's mother to Philine Polak. Original Dutch letter:

"Lieve Philine,

Gistermorgen kwam het vreselijke bericht, dat onze lieve Joop door de Gestapo op 17 April is gefusileerd. Mijn, ònze lieve, lieve schat is heengegaan en gestorven voor haar ideaal. Nooit meer haar te zien, te horen, ook, het is alles zo ontzettend, zo overstelpend, ik kán het je niet beschrijven. Tot ziens.

Veel groeten en een kus van tante Jo en oom P
Wil het s.v.p. aan haar en jouw kennissen, meedelen."

133   Kors, *Hannie Schaft*, 205. Original Dutch letter:

"Beste allemaal,

wat we vreesden is werkelijkheid gebleken: onze enige schat, onze lieve Joop, is door de Gestapobeulen op het allerlaatste ogenblik (17 april waarschijnlijk) om het leven gebracht. We zijn met ontzetting geslagen en ik kan dan ook niet meer schrijven."

134   Official name of the Great Church is: "Grote of St.-Bavokerk" (Great or Saint Bavo Church). This reformed church is located on the Grote Markt in Haarlem and is different from the Catholic Saint Bavo's Cathedral at the Leidschevaart in Haarlem. In order to avoid misunderstandings, I use the name "Great Church" to indicate this reformed church as opposed to the Catholic Saint Bavo's Cathedral.

135   Elsinga, Paul, interview by Sophie Poldermans. (November 6, 2018).

136   Endert, Wim, interviews by Sophie Poldermans. (September and November 2018).

137   Kors, *Hannie Schaft*, 10–14; *De Eerebegraafplaats te Bloemendaal*, Eerebegraafplaats Bloemendaal, October 2018. http://www.eerebegraafplaatsbloemendaal.eu (accessed October 12, 2018).

138   Hammann, *Hannie*, 44.

139   Polak, "Letter from Philine Polak to the National Hannie Schaft Commemoration Foundation," n.d.

140   *Twee zussen in verzet*. Directed by Manon Hoornstra and Thijs Zeeman (MAX, 2016).

141   *Omdat het moet*. Directed by Mieke Benda (National Hannie Schaft Commemoration Foundation, 2014).

142   Elsinga, Paul, interview by Sophie Poldermans. (November 6, 2018).

143   Kors, *Hannie Schaft*, 205.

144   Elsinga, Paul, interview by Sophie Poldermans. (November 6, 2018); Elsinga, "Opening address to the National Hannie Schaft Commemoration of 2012," Haarlem, 2012.

145   Oversteegen, Truus, interviews by Sophie Poldermans. (1998-2016); Elsinga, Paul, interview by Sophie Poldermans. (November 13, 2018); Von Benda Beckmann, *De Velser Affaire*, 2013.

146   Oversteegen, Truus, interviews by Sophie Poldermans. (1998-2016); Elsinga, Paul, interview by Sophie Poldermans. (November 13, 2018).

147   Jacobs, *Palet van verzet*, 138–139.

148   Jacobs, *Palet van verzet*, 138.

149   Jacobs, *Palet van verzet*, 138; Von Benda Beckmann, *De Velser Affaire*, 2013; Braam, *Het schandaal*, 2004.

150   Menger, *Toen Niet, Nu Niet, Nooit*, 205–208.

151   Menger, *Toen Niet, Nu Niet, Nooit*, 205–206.

152   Menger, *Toen Niet, Nu Niet, Nooit*, 205–208; *Andere Tijden. Pantserwagens tegen kransen. Hannie Schaft-herdenking onder vuur*. Directed by Hein Hoffmann (NTR-VPRO, 2010).

153   Oversteegen, Truus, interviews by Sophie Poldermans. (1998-2016); *Andere Tijden. Pantserwagens tegen kransen. Hannie Schaftherdenking onder vuur*. Directed by Hein Hoffmann (NTRVPRO, 2010).

154   Jacobs, *Palet van verzet*, 141–142.

155   Elsinga, Paul, interview by Sophie Poldermans. (November 6, 2018).

156   Oversteegen, Truus, interview by Sophie Poldermans. (February 28, 1998).

157   Hof-Hoogland, and Hof, *Handboek voor globetrotters,* 1993. 137–153.

158   Oversteegen, Truus, interviews by Sophie Poldermans. (1998-2016); Menger, Hannie, interviews by Sophie Poldermans. (1998-2019); and Smithuijsen, "Freddie Oversteegen wilde geen heldin zijn, maar gewoon een méns," October 4, 2018.

159   Jacobs, *Palet van verzet*, 141.

160   Jacobs, *Palet van verzet*, 140–141.

161   Jacobs, *Palet van verzet*, 141.

162   Jacobs, *Palet van verzet*, 141.

163   Jacobs, *Palet van verzet*, 141.

164   *Twee zussen in verzet.* Directed by Manon Hoornstra and Thijs Zeeman (MAX, 2016).

165   Smith, "Freddie Oversteegen, Dutch resistance fighter who killed Nazis through seduction, dies at 92," September 6, 2018.

166   Original Dutch letter:

"Sophie,
Voor ons ben jij de toekomst, de draagster van het nieuwe ideaal, géén racisme, een leefbare wereld!
Dank en liefs,
Truus Menger"

167   Original Dutch letter:

"Veel liefs van
Freddie"

Bibliography

Atwood, Kathryn J. *Women Heroes of World War II. 26 Stories of Espionage, Sabotage, Resistance, and Rescue.* Chicago: Chicago Review Press, 2011.

Hannie Schaft: het meisje met het rode haar. Directed by Ineke Hilhorst. Performed by AVRO. 1980.

Nieuw in Nederland. Performed by AVRO, featuring Sophie Poldermans. 2003.

Bouhuys, M. and P. de Rijcke. *Beeldhouwster Truus Menger.* Hoorn: Stichting Truus Menger Fonds v.d. Beeldende Kunst - Foto's Uitg. i.s.m. Uitgeverij van Spijk. Venlo, 1991.

Braam, Conny. *Het schandaal.* Amsterdam: Uitgeverij Augustus, 2004.

Buitkamp, Jan. *Geschiedenis van het verzet 1940-1945.* Houten: Fibula, 1990.

Bulte, M., and A. Neeven. *Garnizoensstad Haarlem.* The Hague: Tirion Uitgevers, 1992.

Corrie ten Boom House. *The History of the Ten Boom Family.* November 2018. http://www.corrietenboom.com (accessed November 3, 2018).

De Jong, Loe. *De bezetting na 50 jaar.* Vol. 1. The Hague: Sdu Uitgevers, 1990.

—. *Het illegale werk. Fragmenten uit Het Koninkrijk der Nederlanden in de Tweede Wereldoorlog.* The Hague: Staatsuitgeverij, 1977.

De Vries, Theun. *Het meisje met het rode haar.* Amsterdam: Em. Querido's Uitgeverij, 1956.

Eerebegraafplaats Bloemendaal. *De Eerebegraafplaats te Bloemendaal.* October 2018. http://www.eerebegraafplaatsbloemendaal.eu (accessed October 12, 2018).

Elsinga, Paul, interviews by Sophie Poldermans. (1998-2019).

Elsinga, Paul, interview by Sophie Poldermans. (November 6, 2018).

Elsinga, Paul, interview by Sophie Poldermans. (November 13, 2018).

—. "Opening address to the National Hannie Schaft Commemoration of 2012." Haarlem, 2012.

Endert, Wim, interviews by Sophie Poldermans. (September and November 2018).

Geldof, Wilma. *Het meisje met de vlechtjes.* Amsterdam: Luitingh-Sijthoff, 2018.

Hamers, Coen Jr., interview by Sophie Poldermans. (December 12, 2018).

—. *OVERVAL OP Commando-Post (CP) op 16 februari 1945. Een onder-belicht verhaal uit het bezette IJmuiden-Oost.* December 2018. http://www.hamers.nl/genealog/verhalen (accessed December 12, 2018).

Hamers, Coen Sr., and Jo Post, interviews by Sophie Poldermans. (1998-2007).

Hammann, Peter. *Hannie.* Weesp: Uitgeverij In de blije druk, 2017.

Hof-Hoogland, L., and J. Hof. *Handboek voor globetrotters. Twaalf groot-reizigers over hun reizen en ervaringen.* Kampen: Uitgeverij Kok Lyra, 1993.

Jacobs, Simone. *Palet van verzet. Moedige vrouwen toen en nu.* Amsterdam: Boom, 2018.

Jansen, H.P.H., and R. van Riet. *Kalendarium. Geschiedenis van de Lage Landen in jaartallen.* Utrecht: Uitgeverij Het Spectrum, 1971.

Jonker, Ellis. "Freddi and Truus: Sisters in Arms. A Double Portrait of Two Dutch Resistance Fighters in World War II." *Under Fire. Women and World War II. Yearbook of Women's History* 34 (2014): 141-151.

Kloek, Els. "Hannie Schaft. Verzetsvrouw." In *1001 vrouwen in de 20ste eeuw*, by Els Kloek, 1115. Nijmegen: Uitgeverij Vantilt, 2018.

Kors, Ton. *Hannie Schaft. Het levensverhaal van een vrouw in verzet tegen de nazi's.* Amsterdam: Van Gennep, 1980.

Lachman-Polak, Philine, interview by United Sates Holocaust Memorial Museum. (1995).

Twee zussen in verzet. Directed by Manon Hoornstra and Thijs Zeeman. Performed by MAX. 2016.

Menger, Hannie, interviews by Sophie Poldermans. (1998-2019).

Menger, Hannie, interview by Sophie Poldermans. (August 13, 2018).

Menger, Truus. *Op het netvlies van mijn denken.* Westzaan: Uitgeverij Amor Vincit Omnia, 2010.

—. *Toen Niet, Nu Niet, Nooit.* The Hague: Leopold, 1982.

Mulisch, Harry. *De Aanslag.* Amsterdam: Uitgeverij De Bezige Bij, 1982.

National Hannie Schaft Commemoration Foundation. *Fietsen langs het verzet.* Wormerveer, 2004.

Omdat het moet. Directed by Mieke Benda. Performed by National Hannie Schaft Commemoration Foundation. 2014.

Netwerk Oorlogsbronnen. *Bronnen WO2.* October 2018. https://www.oorlogsbronnen.nl (accessed October 12, 2018).

NIOD instituut voor oorlogs-, holocaust- en genocidestudies. October 2018. https://www.niod.nl (accessed October 11, 2018).

North Holland Archives. *Noord-Hollands Archief Beeldbank.* January 2019. https://noord-hollandsarchief.nl/beelden/beeldbank (accessed January 8, 2019).

Andere Tijden. Gewapend verzet. Directed by Yaèl Koren. Performed by NTR-VPRO. 2012.

Andere Tijden. Pantserwagens tegen kransen. Hannie Schaft-herdenking onder vuur. Directed by Hein Hoffmann. Performed by NTR-VPRO. 2010.

Andere Tijden. Steun voor het verzet. Directed by Erik Willems. Performed by NTR-VPRO. 2015.

O'Leary, N. "'Her war never stopped': the Dutch teenager who resisted the Nazis." *The Observer,* September 23, 2018.

Oversteegen, Freddie, interviews by Sophie Poldermans. (1998-2018).

Oversteegen, Truus, interview by Sophie Poldermans. (February 28, 1998).

Oversteegen, Truus, interviews by Sophie Poldermans. (1998-2016).

—. "Letter from Truus Oversteegen to Ms. Koorn." May 20, 1991.

Polak, Philine. "Letter from Philine Polak to the National Hannie Schaft Commemoration Foundation." n.d.

Poldermans, Sophie. *Hannie Schaft. Haar rol in het Nederlandse verzet tijdens de Tweede Wereldoorlog.* Lelystad: AO (Actuele Onderwerpen), 2003.

—. *Seducing and Killing Nazis. Hannie, Truus and Freddie: Dutch Resistance Heroines of WWII.* April 2019. https://www.seducingandkillingnazis. com (accessed April 3, 2019).

—. *Sophie's Women of War.* April 2019. https://www.sophieswomenofwar. com (accessed April 3, 2019).

—. *To all international visitors.* November 2018. https://www.hannieschaft. nl/to-all-international-visitors (accessed November 26, 2018).

Roegholt, R. and J. Zwaan. *Het verzet 1940-1945.* Weesp: Fibula, 1985.

Schaft, Hannie. "Letter from Hannie Schaft to Philine Polak." September 4, 1944.

Schaft, Pieter. "Letter from Pieter Schaft to his family." May 22, 1945.

Schipper, Kees. 2004.

Smith, H. "Freddie Oversteegen, Dutch resistance fighter who killed Nazis through seduction, dies at 92." *Washington Post*, September 6, 2018.

Smithuijsen, D. "Freddie Oversteegen wilde geen heldin zijn, maar gewoon een méns." *NRC Handelsblad*, October 4, 2018.

Het meisje met het rode haar. Directed by Ben Verbong. Performed by Renee Soutendijk. 1981.

Stichting Onderzoek Velser Affaire. *'De Velser Affaire' gepresenteerd.* October 2018. www.velseraffaire.nl/de-velser-affaire-gepresenteerd (accessed October 24, 2018).

Temminck, J. J. *De Haarlemmers en de Tweede Wereldoorlog.* Vol. 7, in *Als de Dag van Gisteren. Honderd jaar Haarlem en de Haarlemmers,* by K.O.H., B.C. Sliggers, B.M.J. Speet, J.J. Temminck, L.J.H. Vroom Daalen, 117-149. Haarlem: Uitgeverij Waanders, 1990.

Ten Boom, C., Sherrill, J., and Sherrill E. *The Hiding Place. The Triumphant True Story of Corrie Ten Boom.* New York: Bantam Books, 1974.

Corrie ten Boom. Het leven van een verzetsheldin. Directed by Neema. Performed by Corrie ten Boom. 2017.

Van der Straaten, H., M. Bulte, F. Koorn, M. Maandag, and E. Vogel. *Bosch en Vaart. Van Heemsteedse buitenplaats naar Haarlems stadskwartier.* Haarlem: De Vrieseborch, 1992.

Van der Wiel, Frans. Melbourne, March 28, 1975.

Van Woerden, Bob (Casper). n.d.

Verzets (Resistance) Museum. *WO2 info.* September 2018. https://www.verzetsmuseum.org/museum/nl/tweede-wereldoorlog (accessed September 2, 2018).

Von Benda Beckmann, Bas. *De Velser Affaire. Een omstreden oorlogsge-schiedenis.* Amsterdam: Boom, 2013.

Vrijer, A. T. J. "Letter from Aafje Talea Johanna Vrijer to Philine Polak." May 22, 1945.

Index

About the Author

SOPHIE POLDERMANS (B. 1981) HAS HAD A FASCINATION for women in war-torn countries from an early age. When she was in high school, she wrote a historical thesis on Hannie Schaft, a Dutch female resistance fighter during the Second World War. At the age of 17, she was the keynote speaker at the National Hannie Schaft Commemoration and appeared in several newspaper, radio and television interviews.

After a year as a foreign exchange student in Sandpoint, Idaho, in the United States, where Sophie also gave speeches on Hannie Schaft at Rotary lunches, she studied both Dutch and International Law at the University of Amsterdam. She specialized in Human Rights and International Criminal Law, with a focus on women. She also holds a degree in Peace and Conflict Studies from the University of California, Berkeley (UC Berkeley) in the United States and a European Master's degree in Human Rights and Democratisation from the European Inter-University Centre for Human Rights (EIUC) in Venice, Italy. She carried out research on Female Genital Mutilation among migrant women in Austria, France, the Netherlands and the United Kingdom at the University of Vienna in Austria. She did an internship at the United Nations International Criminal Tribunal for the former Yugoslavia in The Hague, the Netherlands, where she carried out research on the legal doctrine of "Joint Criminal Enterprise" applied to concentration camp cases in the Second World War and the war in the former Yugoslavia.

Sophie worked as a lecturer in Conflict Resolution at the University of Amsterdam and as a lecturer in International Human Rights and Criminal Law and as an International Coordinator at the Amsterdam University of Applied Sciences for over a decade, serving as a guest lecturer in Madrid, Oslo and virtually in Fukuoka.

Sophie carried out research concerning Transitional Justice in Bosnia-Herzegovina, Kosovo and Rwanda. Her research in Rwanda entailed an exploration of gender and transitional justice with regard to victims of sexual violence during the Rwandan genocide.

She was a board member of the National Hannie Schaft Commemoration Foundation from 2001 to 2011. In 2018, she joined the board again, serving as a member until the present.

She is the author of *Hannie Schaft. Haar rol in het Nederlandse verzet tijdens de Tweede Wereldoorlog* (*Hannie Schaft. Her Role in the Dutch Resistance During the Second World War*), published in the Netherlands in 2003. This book is widely used in high schools.

In addition, she is the author of *Seducing and Killing Nazis. Hannie, Truus and Freddie: Dutch Resistance Heroines of WWII*, published in the United States in 2019.

Sophie Poldermans is a Dutch women's rights advocate. She works as a self-employed author, public speaker, lecturer and consultant on women and war and human rights-related issues from a legal, historical, sociological, anthropological and philosophical perspective and founded Sophie's Women of War (www.sophieswomenofwar.com), an organization that focuses on the role of women during war in the broadest sense of the word.

For inquiries about this book and/or the author; a live or virtual book presentation and/or information about onsite visits to important places in the lives and resistance work of Hannie, Truus and Freddie in Haarlem, please check out the author's website at www.sophieswomenofwar.com or contact the author at info@sophieswomenofwar.com.